Stories Of The Street

Images of the Human Condition

A Police Chaplain's Encounters
With Tragedy, Crime, and Abuse

By

Rev. Steve Best, M.Div.

Volunteer Police Chaplain, Emeritus

Strategic Book Publishing
New York, NewYork

Copyright 2008
All rights reserved – Rev. Steve Best

No part of this book may be reproduced or transmitted in any form or by any means, graphic, electronic, or mechanical, including photocopying, recording, taping, or by any information storage retrieval system, without the permission, in writing, from the publisher.

Strategic Book Publishing
An imprint of AEG Publishing Group
845 Third Avenue, 6th Floor - 6016
New York, NY 10022
www.StrategicBookPublishing.com

ISBN: 978-1-60693-353-4
SKU: 1-60693-353-1

Printed in the United States of America

Book Design: Roger Hayes

Cover Design: Jamie Runyan

Cover Inspiration: The Light shines in the darkness and the darkness does not overcome it.
(John 1:5)

<u>Stories of the Street: Images of the Human Condition</u> honors the daily shift work of law enforcement officers, troopers, and police chaplains who serve the nation's communities with integrity, courage, and compassion.

Table of Contents

Introduction 7
Acknowledgements 13
Preface 15

Street Images I

"They heard the footsteps of God walking."
Genesis 3

1. I've Killed My Baby 21
2. It's Been A Bad Day 29
3. Anxiety Attack 32
4. A Career at Risk 39
5. The Dark Side of Easter 45
6. I Have Sinned 56
7. Feathered Priorities 60
8. The Devil Is in the Details 64

Street Images II

"When I consider the heavens ... the work of thy fingers"
Psalm 8

9. When Bad Things Happen 71
10. An Angel Appears 77
11. Gooseneck Trailers and Grace 84
12. Praying Hands 90

13. Dreaded Dispatch — 92
14. Where Was God Today? — 98

Street Images III

"God make his face to shine upon you and be gracious to you"
Numbers 6

15. The Rookie Cop (Three Parts) — 105

   Part One—Loss of Innocence
   Part Two—Loss of Naiveté
   Part Three—Loss of Family

16. Alcohol, Distraction, and Death — 121

17. Katrina: the Power of Commitment (Five Parts) — 128

   Part One – Commitment upon Personal Loss
   Part Two – Commitment in the Face of Disaster
   Part Three – Commitment by Refusal to Abandon Post
   Part Four – Commitment to Connecting People
   Part Five – Commitment for Sharing Spiritual Things

18. Katrina and Remnant Hope — 139
19. He Spat in My Face — 143
20. Officer Down — 148
21. The Family — 157

Appendix — 167

Introduction

<u>Stories of the Street: Images of the Human Condition</u> is a personal collection of stories I witnessed as a police chaplain on patrol with law enforcement officers and troopers.

My intent in writing these stories is to amplify the variety of incidents to which police patrol officers are dispatched, and to create a better understanding of the role of volunteer police chaplains in their encounters with tragedy, crime, and abuse.

This book is not about the high drama of fast cars and drawn guns found on TV shows like *COPS*, *America's Most Wanted*, *CSI*, and other entertainment venues. Rather, the focus is on the daily shift life and the human emotions of officers and citizens involved in significant and symptomatic events. <u>Stories of the Street: Images of the Human Condition</u> illuminate a normal eight or ten hour police patrol shift that captures and personifies the realities of the street.

The book is intended to provide police families and the community with a broader insight into an average day for a patrol officer serving the nation's communities with honor, courage, and integrity. In addition I am hopeful that the book will create a better understanding of the role volunteer police chaplains serve in law enforcement agencies.

God is present in each story, and the reader is encouraged to find a divine presence in the context of how the reader understands God.

The primary mission for volunteer police chaplain programs is to:

- Provide a comforting presence and spiritual guidance to officers, family members, and civilian staff facing distress
- Respond to officers and families in cases of injury and illness or death
- Serve as the 'on-call' chaplain on a rotating basis
- Counsel officers following critical incidents
- Conduct weddings, baptisms, funerals when requested by police families
- Offer invocations and benedictions for official ceremonies
- Respect all religious denominations and expressions without proselytizing

To qualify as a Police Chaplain, most law enforcement agencies require the following credentials from applicants:

- Be ordained ministers, priests, rabbis or deacons employed in a locally recognized congregational or organizational group
- Applicants must have three or more years experience in parish or congregational ministry
- Provide a letter of endorsement from a judicatory body confirming an applicant's accountability to serve as a police chaplain
- Possess a valid driver's license
- Pass a criminal background check
- Abide by the policies and procedures of the department or agency

Over an eight-year period I was fortunate to serve as a volunteer police chaplain for three law enforcement agencies concurrently. The three departments included a state law enforcement agency, a metropolitan police department, and a suburban police department. Serving three departments as a volunteer chaplain was made possible through the encouragement and the support of the parish I was serving at the time. The parish wanted an outreach program and saw my voluntary police chaplaincy as a vehicle to accomplish their mission.

Voluntary chaplain programs contribute to the emotional and spiritual health of law enforcement officers. The following statements made by leaders of the three departments I served confirm the importance of chaplains to their officers and staff.

Dr. Frances Douglas, Staff Psychologist for the Texas Department of Public Safety (DPS) and supervisor of the volunteer chaplain program commented:

> The Texas Department of Public Safety was established to maintain the public safety of the residents of Texas. DPS Officers take an oath to protect the lives, rights, and property of the residents of Texas. In doing so, he or she assumes a tremendous responsibility. Most make it their life mission to meet this responsibility to the greatest extent possible. How extremely difficult it must be for any law enforcement officer, then, to stand helpless and witness the carelessness of a drunk driver, the senseless violence of an abusive parent, or face the devastation of a natural disaster such as Hurricane Katrina.
>
> Texas DPS Chaplains assist DPS troopers and employees including their families facing the aftermath of life and death situations, both professional and personal, that can severely challenge the mind, body, and spirit. As the Department Administrator of this volunteer program, I have been privileged to witness the tremendous positive impact that the DPS Chaplains have been able to make in assisting our employees who are struggling with difficult times in their lives and careers. Over and over

again, we have observed that most people will recover from adversity with the support of family and friends in the agency and in the larger community. Our chaplains provide guidance, counseling, and assistance to DPS employees, employees' families, victims, and communities in confronting the spiritual, mental, and emotional burdens of crime and disasters. They have my utmost respect and sincerest gratitude for what they do.

Austin (Texas) Police Department Lt. Sharon Voudouris-Ross (Ret) who served as the liaison between "line" (patrol) officers and chaplains wrote:

> When I entered the cadet program of the Austin Police Department (APD) in the late 1970's, our class was the first to have a psychologist assigned to it. The purpose of the psychologist was to administer psychological exams to all cadets to ensure they were mentally and emotionally fit to be a police officer. Later we were to counsel with him if and when we encountered stressors that had the potential to overwhelm us.
> Many of us felt a need for something more. Morning prayer groups were started by officers and civilian personnel to provide support for each other. There was talk about why couldn't the department have a chaplain to help us through personal problems. A new chief was hired. He not only supported the idea of a chaplain, he wanted a chaplain assigned to each police sector in the city.
> The chaplains that came on board knew that they were creating a new era in the department. They also knew they needed to prove themselves to the officers who would be skeptical of trusting them. In our eyes, the chaplains were answerable to a much higher authority than police brass. We knew that what we

heard one-on-one could and would be kept confidential.

The chaplaincy program has been a great success for APD and for the community. The originating chaplains were and are of exceptional caliber. For police officers, chaplains are the extended arms of God to help comfort, teach, direct, listen, and offer compassion and understanding.

Taylor (Texas) Police Chief Jeff Straub expressed his dependence on his volunteer chaplains:

> As a believer, my intent in bringing the volunteer chaplain's program to the police department was to invite God into our organization. In addition, humanistic and community understanding and dialogue were extremely important reasons to bring chaplains into our agency.
>
> Upon establishment of the program, my initial thought was that officers would be reluctant to have a member of the clergy ride with them in their patrol cars or feel that the chaplains were representatives of police administration. I suspected officers would be cynical at worst and extremely cautious at best.
>
> My concerns proved to be unfounded. From the very beginning, officers seemed to welcome the program's ministers and I have never received a single complaint regarding a chaplain's presence.
>
> Initially, my expectations of the program were mild. I thought it would be a positive step for the department, creating at best a support system for them and maybe even allowing respected members of our community (clergy) to see that police officers are different than the stereotypes many people embrace. My expectations have been exceeded beyond measure. The volunteer police chaplains' program in our agency has been a phenomenal source of support,

assistance in community dialogue and has resulted in friendships that will last a lifetime.

Our chaplains have always 'gone above and beyond the call of duty' even offering assistance to victims of crime and assisting in calming scenes where individuals are suffering emotional distress.

The Taylor Police Department's volunteer chaplains' program has been an incredible support mechanism for our employees. They have been there when times were tough and have been there with us to celebrate holidays.

The statements from the three police officials may benefit police departments that are considering volunteer chaplain programs.

Names, locations, sector dispatch codes, and other identifying information in all the stories are fictitious to protect the privacy of police officers, victims of accidents or crime, and citizens involved in a given story. Any similarities between real names, addresses and events in the stories are coincidental.

Lengthy conversations with officers, victims, and citizens are paraphrased.

Pastoral care conversations with police officers and troopers are considered confidential and are not included.

Four-letter words and other profanities common to street talk have been changed to words more acceptable to the reader.

Scripture quotations are from the New Revised Standard Version (NRSV) of the Holy Bible.

Acknowledgements

My appreciation and love for my wife Nancy is infinite. She consistently encouraged my second-career ministry, my commitment to voluntary police chaplaincy, and my writing <u>Stories of the Street: Images of the Human Condition.</u>

I deeply appreciate and am grateful to the officers and troopers of the Austin (Texas) Police Department, Texas Department of Public Safety, and the Taylor (Texas) Police Department for sharing their patrol cars and experiences during ride-outs. The long-term relationships with sworn law enforcement officers formed over my years as a police chaplain have given me faith that our society is more holistic because of their routine shift work in our communities.

Special acknowledgement is given to Police Chief Jeff Staub, Dr. Frances Douglas, PSY.D, Lt. Sharon Voudouris-Ross (Ret), and Patrol Officer Amy Gonzales. I also value Suzanne Butterfield's contribution of two poems that magnify the pain the law enforcement community feels in a line-of-duty death.

I am grateful for the help and encouragement from my dear friends and advisors: retired publisher Jason Petosa who provided conceptual guidance and edits of the text; and attorney Judy Osborn who fine-tuned the stories. I am also thankful to Rev./Dr. Darrel Gilbertson for his contribution to the theological structure of the book.

Rev. Steve Best

Immanuel and Prince of Peace Lutheran Parish of Taylor, Texas encouraged and supported my volunteer police chaplaincy while I served as pastor to the Parish. Their mission of outreach to the broader community and to law enforcement is respected and admired.

Preface

> The young officer stops at the exit gate of the police substation. He begins his shift with this prayer:
>
> Lord, bless my mission tonight,
> That I may be fair and respectful to everyone I meet tonight,
> That I may use wisdom in my judgments,
> That I have courage to do my job in difficult circumstances.
>
> Be with my family while I am away,
> Keep them safe,
> Keep me safe and,
> Return me safely to them at shift's end.
>
> In Jesus' name I pray. Amen.

This book is based on responses by police officers to everyday occurrences in the lives of citizens. Some are tragic in nature, some are criminal acts perpetuated by those who live outside the laws of society, and some are routine. All have theological overtones.

Rev. Steve Best

I asked Rev./Dr. Darrel Gilbertson:

Where is God in these stories?
What theological reflections do you discover in the stories?

Dr. Gilbertson replied:

This is a book about hope. We define hope as courage under fire. And we also insist hope is both attitude and action. And that hope, like love, never quits.

I am drawn to these stories by their poignancy – a combination of a window to the hard edges of human existence but also a helicopter view of the bigger police or law enforcement picture.

As a pastor for over four decades, I ache for the people who live out these tales of triumph and defeat. As a pastor, I also honor the people who lay their lives on the line daily. They offer care and help (in some cases it is to help protect people from their own self-destructive habits and behavior).

At Dr. Gilbertson's suggestion, the stories are grouped in ways in which law enforcement and human activity reflect the human condition.

Street Images One describe the innate cultural and religious temperament out of which guilt and folly arise. Genesis 3: *"They heard the footsteps of God walking."*

Street Images Two describe the often faint but still legible handwriting and signature of God's presence. In Psalms 8: *"When I consider the heavens...the work of thy fingers."*

Street Images Three describe the awesome face-to-face encounters that inspire the words *hero/heroine, miracle worker, grace, vocation, career, ministry, compassion, sacramental*, and *"angelic."* The Old Testament Book of Numbers, Chapter 6 says: *"God blesses us and keeps us, God makes his face shine upon us and is gracious to us. God looks upon us with favor and gives us peace."* By mutual love we may have entertained angels without knowing it.

It is my hope that readers experience God's Presence in <u>Stories of the Street: Images of the Human Condition</u>.

Street Images I

"They heard the footsteps of God walking."

Genesis 3

1

"I've Killed My Baby"

Yolanda and Anita are driving home on a beautiful spring afternoon. Yolanda is at the wheel of her SUV on the service road of an expressway, intending to merge onto a southbound lane. In the back of the large vehicle are seven children – Yolanda's four children, ages three through seven, and Anita's three children, ages four through eleven.

Yolanda is driving fast, hoping to beat the afternoon congestion that always clogs the local expressways in evening rush hour traffic.

With seven kids in the back seats of the SUV, grabs and arguments among the children are inevitable. As the vehicle approaches the entrance ramp, Yolanda turns to correct the children and tell them to be quiet. The children are not wearing seat belts.

Yolanda returns her attention to the road and realizes that the traffic in front of her has stopped. She jerks the steering wheel hard to the right, trying desperately to avoid a small red pickup truck. The SUV goes into a yaw and rolls over into a six-foot black metal tubing fence. Anita's oldest child, eleven-year-old Sylvia, is thrown out of the vehicle by the centrifugal force of the spinning vehicle. Her head and shoulders are contorted from being propelled through the metal fence. Adding to the gruesome scene is the SUV resting upside down on the lower half of Sylvia's small body.

Sylvia is dead.

The driver of the pickup truck jumps out and runs to the overturned vehicle. Horrified by what he sees, he returns to his truck and flees. Obviously the accident was not his fault; nevertheless, he flees the scene without anyone capturing his license plate number.

Rookie Police Officer Ernie is the first to arrive at the accident site. He finds Sylvia's mother, Anita, screaming and trying to free her impaled child from the fence and from under the SUV. Her efforts are to no avail.

Other officers and emergency medical service (EMS) vehicles arrive within minutes. An EMS technician covers Sylvia's lifeless body with a blue plastic tarp. Miraculously, Yolanda, Anita, and the remaining six children are unhurt. They are moved to two ambulances, one with Yolanda and her four children, the other with Anita's two remaining children.

I am on a ride-along that day with Officer John. We are in a shopping mall parking lot, working a minor traffic accident. John is following routine police procedures for private property auto accidents – officers are not required to write tickets or assign blame. John has retrieved two sets of "blue forms" from the trunk of his patrol car to hand out to the two parties involved in the fender bender.

John's patrol unit radio sounds out dispatch and officer transmissions about the fatal accident that has just occurred on the southbound expressway service road. The first responding officer, Ernie, reports a "Sig 2," meaning a deceased female at the scene.

Back inside the patrol car John remarks; "Damn it! Here I am with a chaplain on board and I am working this meaningless fender bender. We need to get you to the fatality." Just then another officer pulls into the parking lot and John asks her to take charge of the parking lot incident "so that I can get the Chaplain to the Sig 2." The backup officer readily agrees.

We are running code three – overhead strobe lights of red, blue, and white. The patrol unit's siren screams its warning for civilian cars to get out of the way. The high-speed ride is periodically jolted by ear-piercing blasts of the patrol unit's air horn directed at motorists who do not respond to our flashing lights and siren.

We reach the expressway service road. It is barricaded to prevent any traffic from blundering into the chaotic scene a block away. John approaches the officer manning the barricade and hits his bullhorn microphone and tells the blockade officer to let us through: "I have the chaplain on board." The attending officer waves us through.

We park a short distance away from two ambulances and start walking. Following police chaplain protocol I ask John "to take me to the officer in charge" to discern if and where he needs me. Instead John announces in his authoritative voice, "The Chaplain is here!" and proceeds to march me to the center of activity at the rear doors of the ambulances.

The scene is surreal. Rush-hour traffic crawls as rubberneckers peer in disbelief at the carnage and the flashing strobe lights on the emergency vehicles.

The eyes of the first responders, including their supervisors, turn toward me as if in slow motion. They have a look that seems to say; "Help us, Chaplain". In reality no one is speaking. They just stare at me for what seems a lifetime.

I am conscious of the roar coming from the two ambulances' diesel engines. Each ambulance faces the tragic sight of the upside-down SUV with its contents strewn over the roadside and with little Sylvia's contorted body pinned beneath its bulk.

Calmly, pointing to the ambulance directly in front of me, I ask the EMS supervisor; "Who is in this ambulance?"

He replies, "The driver and her kids."

I point to the second ambulance and ask the same question: "Who is in that one?"

"The children of the dead girl's mother."

"Where is the mother?"

He points to the space between the two ambulances. He says; "She's right there. We are trying to get her into the ambulance with her children. Her little boy is so scared that he continues to throw up. She won't go. She is frantic to hold her daughter."

Between the ambulances stand a female police officer and a young EMS technician. They are talking to Anita in low tones. She is attempting to run to her precious Sylvia lying dead less than fifty feet away. The female officer and EMS technician are doing their best to keep her from seeing the covered body. They want to move her into the ambulance with her remaining two children.

I join in the effort to convince Anita that her surviving children need her to be with them. Anita's motherly instinct is to rescue her first-born child. I am reminded of Jesus' words; *Which one of you, having a hundred sheep and losing one of them, does not leave the ninety-nine in the wilderness and go after the one that is lost until he finds it?* [1]

In desperate and frantic struggles to break free, Anita wails with gut-wrenching outbursts, "I have to hold my baby! She is afraid of strangers. She is afraid to be alone. I can't leave her alone like this!" She is gasping for air as fatigue and shock begin to overwhelm her. Anita is in full denial that her Sylvia is dead.

Two experienced female Victim Services personnel arrive and join efforts to calm Anita. Given their training and experiences with trauma victims, they slowly and cautiously move Anita into the waiting ambulance. Looking inside, I see the terrified faces of two young children, faces that remain frozen in my memory.

I turn my attention to the ambulance sheltering Yolanda and her children. I enter the rear doors and see an EMS technician sitting on the right side of the unit. She is taking

---

[1] Luke 15:4 - NRSV

vital signs and medical information from Yolanda. The technician looks up from her chart and smiles. She tells me that the seven-year-old boy sitting in front of her was responsible for getting the surviving children out of the overturned vehicle. "Chaplain, Hector was a real hero today. He got his family out of the car." I smile at Hector and thank him.

I sit down opposite Yolanda. She is crying in desperate sobs. Through her tears she notices the gold crosses on the collar of my police uniform. She begins to moan in deepening grief; "I have killed my baby. Sylvia is my favorite niece and the oldest. She loves me, and I love her. I have killed my baby! I have killed my baby! My sister will hate me."

I respond; "Yolanda, I have been with Anita and she is not saying anything about being angry at you. That is something you do not need to worry about. Take care of your children here. They need you."

Yolanda opens her heart to the fact that life the past few days has been harsh for her, Anita, and their children. "My children's father left yesterday for prison. He will be gone a long time. Our mother kicked us out of her house. We have nowhere to go. We have no money. And now this! My kids have lost their dad and now their Sylvia."

Yolanda looks at her children. One is the seven-year-old boy who was being attended to by the technician. Pointing at the child she reminds me: "Hector saved us. He got us all out of the car. He is our hero."

I look at Hector's tear-stained face. "Hector, we are all very proud of you. You really are a hero and you did all the right things to help your family. I am very proud of you too."

Without warning the rear doors of the ambulance open and the driver of the EMS announces, "It is time to go!" He nods at me, indicating that I should exit the ambulance. I take Yolanda's hand, give a hug, and step down out of the ambulance.

My compassion for these two women and their six remaining children has totally consumed my emotions and physical energy.

The Crime Scene Investigators (CSI) have taken command of the investigation of the fatal wreck, a routine matter when a death has occurred. Yellow tape forms a large circle around the overturned SUV and the covered body of young Sylvia. Police photographers are recording the scene.

The mood is somber as Officer John and I walk back to our police cruiser.

I ask John, "Are you OK?"

"Oh, yeah! I was a Marine before becoming a police officer. I have seen a lot of death in my time. This doesn't bother me at all."

I thought to myself, "If it doesn't bother you, then why are we not driving back to our assigned sector? Why are we heading toward the hospital? We are no longer a part of the triage. The emergency room personnel and the victim services staff have taken over. Why are we going to the hospital?" Only my thoughts – I do not ask.

John parks outside the ER room at the trauma hospital. As we enter the triage area, I am summoned to Yolanda's curtained cubicle. An investigating police officer tells me Yolanda is talking about suicide and asks if I would talk with her.

Now I know why God moved John to come here.

Opening the curtain, I step inside and approach her gurney. I take her hand and bring it into my folded hands:

> Merciful God, we come to you with broken hearts. We cry for young Sylvia and for this family. We lift up Sylvia, that you receive her into your arms with love and adoration. We pray for Yolanda – that she may be free from her despair. We pray for Anita and her family that they will find the strength to face each day with the courage to somehow accept those things we do not understand. We pray these things in the name of Jesus. Amen.

Tears trickle down Yolanda's cheeks. Even in the face of such a devastating tragedy for her and her family, a temporary sense of peace seems to come over her. I continue to hold her hand as we both contemplate the disaster before us.

The curtain opens and a Highway Enforcement Officer enters the cubicle with clipboard and pen in hand. It's time to record the reality of the day.

Before leaving the hospital, I make sure the ER charge nurse has called the hospital chaplain. She assures me she has paged him and he is on the way. The family is gathering in an upstairs waiting room and they will need his help during the hours that follow.

"Nope, doesn't bother me," John says as we pass the accident scene on the way back to our sector. "Doesn't bother me at all. Look! The Crime Scene Investigation (CSI) Team is still there. She (Sylvia) is still under that car."

Four times that night, before the shift change at 2:00 a.m., we leave our designated sector and drive by the scene to "see if the area has cleared."

"Nope – doesn't bother me at all!"

But the death scene does bother Ernie, the first officer to arrive at the accident scene. He is solemn and withdrawn from his shift mates. He tells me the details of little Sylvia being "grated like a piece of cheese" through the metal fence. He talks in a soft voice as he looks at the floor, reliving his moments alone with the hysterical mother. He questions if he did the right thing in removing Anita from the horrific and blood-drenched setting to a place that would provide privacy and security.

The death of a child weighs heavily on the hearts of first responders. Police officers, EMS personnel, fire personnel, victim services personnel, and police chaplains are often the first ones on the scenes of horrific accidents or traumatic violence involving children. Even though they must set aside personal feelings while serving the victims and the families, the death of a child will preoccupy their thoughts and emotions for hours, days, or even weeks.

Rev. Steve Best

Without exception, when you ask a police officer what he or she dreads most in their duties, the answer will always be: "The injury or death of a child."

First responders mentally replay the horrible scenes they witness. Sometimes, a first responder will pay more attention and give more affection to his or her own children following an incident involving a child. Sometimes, the first responder will suffer mental and emotional fatigue resulting in depression that in turn may lead to alcoholism or other abuses.

Without a formal Critical Incident Stress Management (CISM) debriefing therapy rookie Ernie will have to depend on his shift partners, his family, and himself to vet any feelings of depression and despair that invariably leads to sleepless nights, impatience with family and associates, and job fatigue. (Reference Appendix)

I encourage him to call me. He never does. Neither does he return my call.

I keep a picture from a newspaper on my desk of rescue personnel working to remove the bodies of a young mother and her little girl from a crushed vehicle. Standing off to the side of the rescue team is a police officer pensively watching the rescue. There is visible pain in his face as he watches the recovery of the little girl's lifeless body from the crushed wreckage. The picture is strikingly powerful. The young officer's posture suggests he is visualizing his own child in such a tragedy.

The pain is too much to bear.

2

"It's Been a Bad Day"

Senior Patrol Office (SPO) Chub is four hours into his evening shift that began at 4:30 p.m. We are patrolling an area filled with low-income housing and known for its drug culture and its accompanying prostitution.

The night is cool for late June, and our conversation is casual. Without warning, Chub makes a tight U-turn on the darkened narrow street, floors the accelerator, and hits his overheads (lights) in full pursuit of a small dark-colored sedan.

"What's the deal?" I ask. Chub quips: "Only one headlight."

The sedan approaches an intersection with a convenience store on the corner. We pull in behind the car with our overheads splashing red, blue, and white colors on the outside wall of the store. Because of the history of the neighborhood, a back-up unit pulls onto the apron of the parking lot in front of the sedan.

The sedan stops. The passenger door bursts open and a high school age boy jumps out of the car. In a dead run he heads toward a vacant lot. As he enters the dark field, he tosses something into the tall grass. The back-up officer, Ken, takes off in a hot pursuit foot chase.

SPO Chub immediately turns his attention to the woman inside the stopped vehicle. He approaches the driver side door, yells at the woman; "Driver! Turn your engine off!" The woman turns her ignition and the engine stops.

"Put both hands on the steering wheel where I can see them!" The driver responds and we soon see the driver is a White middle age female.

"Get out of your vehicle; keep your back toward me! Put your hands up where I can see them!" She does.

"Move to the rear of your car and put your hands on the trunk." She obeys.

Chub approaches the woman, takes one arm and then the other, pulls the arms behind the woman, and handcuffs her.

All of these actions are dutifully being recorded on the video camera in Chub's patrol car.

Radio chatter is constant as the pursuing officer, Ken, yells into his mike the direction he and the running suspect are headed. Other patrol units seem to appear from nowhere. A perimeter is instantly established to confine the youth in a defined search area. Within minutes, Ken emerges from the field with the youth handcuffed. Ken tightly holds the back of the youth's muscle shirt. The high-school-age young man is taken to Ken's patrol car and placed in the back seat. He will be taken to a juvenile detention center for processing in the justice system.

The item the youth threw into the tall grass is recovered, and to no one's surprise, it is a "baggie of rocks" – crack cocaine.

Examination of the female's ID reveals her name, date of birth, address, city, and state. Cynthia is 42 years old. She lives in a high-income section of the city and is miles away from home.

Strewn throughout the back seat of Cynthia's late-model sedan are a child's safety seat, white cotton underwear, and other clothing that indicates Cynthia is the mother of at least one young child under the age of four. On the driver's side of the front seat are her husband's business cards disclosing he is a vice president of a national high-tech company.

Cynthia is arrested for possession of crack cocaine and contributing to the delinquency of a minor. She remains handcuffed and is placed in the back seat of our patrol unit for transport to the county jail. She will be charged with possession of a controlled substance and endangerment of a child – the teenage boy.

On the way to jail, the heavy and repulsive smell of crack cocaine saturates the patrol car. To add to the alien smell, Cynthia repeatedly says in a monotone voice, as if speaking only to herself, "It's been a bad day. It's been a bad day."

She is so right.

On the way back to our sector from the jail, Chub comments on the cross-pollination of disillusioned wealth and disadvantaged hopelessness that kiss each other in the common addiction to crack cocaine. "I see this happen over and over again in this community. The prostitution for crack will continue; the chases of young men will continue; the arrests will be an every-night occurrence.

"Nothing changes."

3

Anxiety Attack

The monthly chaplains' meeting is over and I am visiting with one officer when I am summoned by another to help a woman in distress. The woman came to the police station to report an incident of road rage that had happened only moments earlier.

Gloria was taking her two boys to school when a young man driving a pickup truck began to tailgate her vehicle. She was approaching the school zone and dropped her speed to the required 20 miles per hour. When Gloria signaled a left turn into the school driveway, the man sped past her on the right, giving her a vulgar hand gesture. Minutes later, she saw the same vehicle in a service station. She wrote down the license plate number and drove to the police station to report the incident.

Gloria tells her story to two officers at police headquarters. The officers write down the details of her story and tell her how they appreciate her attention to detail in getting the description and the license number of the violator. Gloria stands to leave when, without warning, she breaks down in tears. She shows far greater emotion than what the traffic incident would warrant. She explains to the police officers that she has just found out that her dad had been found dead in an apartment in another city. For reasons she does not yet know, the police in that city had declared the apartment a crime scene. The father had lived alone and apparently had been dead several days before he was discovered.

Knowing that I am in the building, the interviewing officers ask that I come to help calm the young mother. After listening to her stories, and assuring her that the police department was there to help her, Gloria leaves to continue her unpredictable day. I give her my cell phone number and offer to visit with her if she feels the need.

Within hours of the road rage incident police officers track the license plate of the road rage perpetrator. He is arrested and charged with reckless driving and the endangerment of a child. The young man has outstanding warrants on other traffic violations. He is jailed.

For the police it appears the incident is just another day in the routine of serving the community. But it isn't.

About 9:30 that evening my cell phone rings. I answer it and hear Gloria pleading for help. She asks me to come to her home. Her voice clearly indicates that she is in distress. It is highly unusual for a police chaplain to be called out by a citizen, especially to come to the citizen's home.

Recognizing the request has associated risks, I call police dispatch and notify them of the call-out. I alert the dispatcher to move a patrol unit into Gloria's neighborhood should I need backup. I dress in my police chaplain uniform and drive to Gloria's home.

As I approach the front door I hear a woman's voice screaming and wailing. The door opens just as I step onto the porch. A young man in his mid-20s stands there with a look of fear and bewilderment. Inside, on the living room couch is Gloria. Wailing, flinging arms and legs, she is out of control. She is hyperventilating.

I ask the young man; "What is your name?"

"Manny."

"Are you Gloria's son?" I ask, taking note of the obvious age difference between Gloria and Manny.

"No, sir. I am her boyfriend."

"Manny, go get a towel, rinse it in cold water and bring it to me."

"Yes, sir."

Manny quickly returns with a wet towel.

Wiping Gloria's face with the cold towel with one hand, I call 911 on my cell phone with the other hand. I request an EMS unit and for the police backup (that I hope is in place). In between trying to calm Gloria down with the cold compresses, I instruct Manny to "go outside and flag down the EMS and police units" when they turn the corner some 150 yards away.

Within minutes, both EMS and police are there and attending Gloria. Immediately EMS technicians take her vital signs. It is determined she is having an acute anxiety attack. Because she remains in an uncontrollable state — screaming and kicking — she is restrained, placed in the ambulance and taken to the hospital.

My attention is drawn to two young boys, approximately nine and 12 years old. They are standing in the hallway with looks of fear and abandonment. I go over to them, bend down and take their small hands.

"Boys, your Mom will be OK. She is crying because she has had a very hard day. Do you understand?" They nod in agreement, but say nothing.

"Manny, you must stay in this house with the boys until you find a relative or neighbor to care for them. Whatever you do, do NOT leave them alone!"

"Yes, sir."

I exit the house and follow the ambulance to the hospital.

Gloria is in the emergency room, still restrained but struggling and crying uncontrollably. Although she is hooked up to an IV, the medicine has not had time to calm her acute anxiety. When the attending nurses see me, they acknowledge my presence and then leave Gloria's bedside. I find myself alone with Gloria in the small ER room.

She does not seem to hear, or want to hear, anything I am telling her. She moves her head from side to side in quick rotations as if trying to escape the reality of the moment. Words of comfort and assurance do not overcome the surges of anxiety and hopelessness.

Moments pass. I wonder, "What do I do next?"

Then I remember when I was a little boy and was afraid of anything, my mother would come to my side, stroke my head, and sing *Jesus Loves Me*.

"Gloria, do you know the song *Jesus Loves Me, This I Know*?"

Gloria's look indicates she does.

"Would you like to hear it?"

She nods her head up and down.

In a low voice I begin the song while gently stroking her forehead with my hand.

> Jesus loves me, this I know,
> For the Bible tells me so.
> Little ones to him belong,
> They are weak but he is strong.
> Yes, Jesus loves me;
> Yes, Jesus loves me;
> Yes, Jesus loves me,
> For the Bible tells me so.[2]

As I sing and then hum the song, Gloria gently moves her head in unison with the melody. Not surprisingly, Gloria begins to quiet down and soon falls asleep. This is a *holy moment* with just the two of us in the small ER room with all its life-saving equipment. It is the love of Jesus that prevails in bringing peace to Gloria, and to me as well. My own anxiety of the past hour and a half is suddenly released in the song.

---

[2] Anna Bartlett Warner, 1859; William Batchelder Bradbury, 1861 – The Presbyterian Hymnal: Hymns, Psalms, and Spiritual Songs, Westminster/John Knox Press, Louisville, KY, 1990, Hymn #304

I pray over Gloria and bless her with the Blessing of Aaron:

> Now may the Lord bless you and keep you.
> May He make his face shine upon you,
> And be gracious unto you.
> May He look upon you with favor,
> And give you His peace.[3]

Gloria is asleep.
I step outside the room into the hospital hallway.
Manny has arrived at the hospital. A neighbor has taken the boys to her house for the night. Nurses tell me they have reached Gloria's mother in another city and that she is on the way. Soon those who love her will nourish Gloria.
All is calm. The nurses thank me for assisting them, and I leave for home.
What is behind this anxiety? We know that the road rage incident was the trigger, but what is the core issue in Gloria's life that caused such extreme reactions?
Following Gloria's release from the hospital a few days later, she calls me and asks me to come counsel with her about her ordeal, including how she should handle her deceased father's funeral. We sit on her living room couch, the same couch on which she suffered her attack, and she begins to tell me her story.
She remembers her father leaving the family when she was a young girl. As a result she knew little of his whereabouts or lifestyle. The sudden and unexpected news of her father's death the morning of the road-rage incident carries an additional dark side that disturbs her deeply.
A police official from an out-of-area department had called her with the news that her father was a convicted pedophile with several convictions and jail terms.

---

[3] Numbers 6:24-26 - NRSV

Stories Of The Street

In his seventies, the father had died of natural causes alone in his apartment. Unfortunately, he was not discovered for almost a week after his death. In his apartment was a large collection of pornographic magazines and videotapes. The police designated the apartment as a crime scene and confiscated all his belongings. Because Gloria was his daughter, his ashes were sent to her against the volatile wishes of other relatives on her father's side of the family. The dispute over the ashes had compounded Gloria's emotional distress.

Gloria acknowledged his rejection of her and her mother. She was saddened by his pedophile pathology, his prison record, and the presence of pornography in his apartment that authenticate his addiction to sex. Despite all of these issues, Gloria retained genuine love and compassion for her dad. She wanted to respectfully inter his remains.

Listening to her sincerity, I suggested that I bless her father's ashes sitting unobtrusively on the coffee table in front of us. Looking at the unadorned cremains urn, I could not help but think that the vessel and its contents seemed to have been given a sense of dignity through Gloria's love and forgiveness.

Holding my hand over the urn, I blessed the ashes, praying a prayer for God's grace over this fallen human being. "In the sure and certain hope of the resurrection to eternal life through our Lord Jesus Christ, we commend to almighty God, Alberto, and we commit his ashes to their final resting place." I made the sign of the cross over the urn and took Gloria's hand in an act of sympathy.

Gloria had been raised Catholic but was not active in the local Catholic parish. She felt, however, a strong responsibility to have her father's life acknowledged and reconciled with the church. I encouraged her to call the neighborhood parish priest and arrange a formal Catholic Rite for the Dead ceremony. Several days later the local newspaper listed Gloria's father's name in its obituary column along with the time of his funeral service at the Catholic parish.

My experience with Gloria is the only time during my ministry as a police chaplain that I was called out to minister to

Rev. Steve Best

a private citizen. A police chaplain's primary mission is to care for officers and their families. The episode with Gloria is also the only time that I have been the first responder on scene for a "critical incident" — a hysterical and out-of-control person.

Looking back on the events at Gloria's home and at the hospital, I am thankful for God's presence that made me available to minister to a person during a personal crisis. I am also thankful for the many hours of police training that enabled me to respond in a professional manner.

4

A Career at Risk

Have you ever wondered why people with a good education and excellent career opportunities often put themselves and their future at risk? To risk the investment of time, energy, and money in achieving professional status is outside the boundaries of ordinary temptations and behavior.

Jonathan is just such a professional. He is wearing surgical greens. He is exceedingly well groomed and is wearing new Nike running shoes. But police have abruptly taken him from his Mercedes Benz. Jonathan is being held in a police command center for transport to the county jail. He was arrested for soliciting an undercover police officer for sex. What led him to risk his personal life and career?

Moral and ethical standards are taught us by our parents and reinforced during the educational phase of a professional career. These standards are mandated through the process of maturing as students seek a professional career in disciplines such as medicine, law, engineering, accounting, or ministry. What temptations have the power to draw people outside the boundaries of their core values and to place at risk their professional career opportunities?

The professional man or woman is not exempt from the same temptations to which the rest of society is vulnerable. Greed, arrogance, addiction, and lust are part and parcel of the Seven Deadly Sins[4] that erode the ethical and spiritual health of people. The erosion of professional ethical values brings with it severe penalties and personal loss, if not disgrace.

Professionals may well see themselves as having Teflon protection that enables them to escape the discipline of their profession, the laws of society, and/or the criticism of their peers and community in general. In reality they do not have a Teflon shield, or any other kind.

Jonathan, our professional in surgical greens, finds himself in custody as a result of a community policing initiated sting operation.

The concept of community policing is founded on the principle of officers and citizens working together to reduce crime in a specific neighborhood. Law enforcement community outreach programs help create trust and interaction between the citizens of a community and a police department.

Input from citizens and local businesses is a critical ingredient in community policing. Without community input, locating and shutting down habitual nuisances such as criminal mischief, drug activity, and prostitution would be much more difficult.

When citizens report reoccurring incidents of criminal activity, police units called Street Response Teams are assigned to investigate and address the criminal activity. In order to prosecute "street crimes" such as prostitution and illicit drug trafficking, specific violations must be observed. Police departments that set up sting operations for prostitution and drug transactions must be able to document their arrests through a variety of ways.

Stings apprehend those participating in illicit activities by catching them in a well-planned and executed net. Most sting

---

[4] The Roman Catholic Church divides sin into two principal categories: venial (minor sin) and capital or mortal sin. The Seven Deadly Sins are mortal sins. They are: pride, avarice, lust, anger, gluttony, envy, and sloth.

operations are initiated through complaints from residents and/or businesses of a specific neighborhood – a direct result of community policing.

A sting operation to stop prostitution is called a "john sting." A "john" is the client or customer of a prostitute. In a "john sting" female police officers pose as prostitutes in an area either known for its prostitution or reported by neighborhood citizens.

The primary objective of a "john sting" is to respond to criminal activity in a given neighborhood by arresting persons making offers of money or other remuneration in exchange for sexual acts that violate city ordinances.

Each law enforcement agency has its own policies and procedures in formulating a "john sting" in a specific area. There are, however, certain basic components to which most agencies generally adhere. The collaborative pieces usually consist of:

- a specific area known for criminal activity
- a team of sworn officers with specific assignments within the sting plan of operation
- undercover officers who play roles most likely to attract criminal activity
- back-up personnel in disguise to provide immediate aid should an uncover officer be in danger
- hidden video or recording equipment to document the criminal transaction
- patrol units to transport offenders away from the scene
- a command center that process arrested offenders and coordinates their transport to city jail

In this story, a 60-foot strip of sidewalk in an area known for prostitution was chosen for a "john sting". Nearby a nondescript police vehicle video records johns who approach and solicit a female police officer posing as a prostitute.

The monitoring vehicle has clear visual access to the designated strip of sidewalk. The female officer is dressed in non-suggestive clothing. Her demeanor suggests she is available to males seeking sexual favors.

To minimize the risk of violence against the undercover officer, a second officer is positioned in close proximity. The back up officer poses as a transient and/or a local drunk. He is shabbily dressed and obviously unkempt. He places a wine bottle on the bench next to him that enhances his disguise. He is hardly noticeable.

Staged several blocks away are unmarked police units. When a john makes a verbal solicitation for sex, usually from his car, the undercover female officer sends a prearranged signal to the observation team in the parked vehicle. They radio the staged patrol units that a "hit" has occurred.

Immediately Street Response units converge on the surprised john and arrest him. The john is quickly removed from his vehicle and placed into an unmarked police car and taken to a command center several blocks from the arrest scene.

At the time the john is arrested, another officer on the arrest team commandeers the john's vehicle and drives it away from the scene and to the command center. The vehicle is impounded with other seized vehicles collected during the sting operation.

Both the arrested john and his vehicle are removed so fast that the average citizen will not even notice the drama. The immediacy of the arrest is to prevent compromising the physical setup of the sting area.

Following the arrest, the female undercover officer gets into an unmarked backup unit, leaving the area vacant except for the police observation car and the disguised back-up officer at the bus stop. Another female undercover officer is placed on scene and the sting operation waits for the next john to appear. It usually doesn't take long before the scenario repeats itself.

At the command center, johns are identified, photographed, fingerprinted, and interviewed. They sit in a designated area of the command center, facing the wall with the other arrested johns awaiting transport to the county jail.

Their cars, parked outside the command center, will be towed to a wrecking yard for retrieval the next day. The john is responsible for the towing and impoundment fees.

The arresting female undercover officers are also taken to the Street Response Command Center where they write detailed reports of each john's verbal offer of sex for money. These reports are legal documents used by a judge for prosecuting prostitution.

Jonathan is caught in a "john sting" that was set up in a neighborhood consisting primarily of blue-collar workers and laborers. These men drive pickup trucks and vans loaded with tools of their trades.

In this setting Jonathan appears. It is about 9:30 p.m. He drives up to the female officer in an expensive Mercedes Benz. He engages her in a discussion of various sexual acts he fantasizes about. Standard to form, he makes a verbal offer for a specific sex act. The officer gives the predetermined signal, the arresting units converge, and Jonathan is taken to the command center for processing. His Mercedes is driven to the collection area and placed among the pickup trucks, vans, and older model vehicles. The Mercedes stands in stark contrast to its more utilitarian associates.

What makes this an interesting case is Jonathan's clothes. He is wearing surgical greens. He is exceedingly well groomed and is wearing new Nike running shoes. He is an aberration among the day workers being held for transport to the county jail. Jonathan is the only professional career person in the command center's holding pen.

During his subsequent identification, photographing, fingerprinting, and interview, I hear Jonathan say, "What am I going to tell my fiancée?"

Consider Jonathan. He is a person of professional training. He has reached a high level of financial success as evidenced by his expensive car and his top-of-the-line shoes. Does he not recognize the type of neighborhood he is in, in contrast to his own life style? Is he willing to risk being infected with the long-term dangers of HIV and other sexually transmitted diseases? Is he willing to risk his career and his relationship with his bride-to-be?

In the choices he makes in this moment, Jonathan voids his entire value system – his integrity, trustworthiness, commitment, and honesty. He places at risk a financially rewarding career in the field of medicine. Apparently he in denial of the risk of arrest and the certain criticism and rejection by his family, professional peers, and his devastated fiancée.

> *What comes out of the mouth proceeds from the heart, and this is what defiles. For out of the heart come evil intentions…adultery, fornication, [and] false witness…These are what defile a person.*[5]

On the other hand, many of Jonathan's arrested mates did not put at risk the loss of income. Other than the fines imposed by the justice system for prostitution, and the fees to recover their trucks, they are not likely to lose their jobs because of their arrests.

What about the undercover police women playing the role of prostitutes? To me they appeared to function in a virtual reality. It was obvious they found the john solicitations offensive and disgusting, an affront to their moral values and the sanctity of their marriage vows or personal relationships.

The genre of this book is about the daily shift work of sworn police officers. The "john sting" is not about fast cars and big guns. It is not about SWAT responses to high profile violence. "John stings" are about immorality and licentiousness present in the works of darkness.

---

[5] Matthew 15:18,19 - NRSV

5

The Dark Side of Easter

Christians consider Easter Sunday a blessed event. Easter: the centerpiece of our faith and hope, and confirmation of God's promise of a Savior to heal the world. Christians who are active in their faith attend Passion Week services including Ash Wednesday, Maundy Thursday, Good Friday, and the Saturday Midnight Easter Vigil.

Then on Easter Sunday we rise to Mary Magdalene's glorious discovery of the Risen Lord. We come rejoicing. We are overwhelmed by majestic and conquering music. We sing with one voice *Jesus Christ Is Risen Today*.

The minister or priest announces "He is Risen!" and congregations respond in unison and with exuberant voices; "He is Risen Indeed!"

In contrast to the Light of Christ shining so brightly on Easter Sunday, there exists another world only a short distance away from the joy and happiness of the Risen Lord. There is blindness to the presence of the sacred.

When I entered police chaplaincy, I was told that the two most active days for family and domestic violence were Easter Sunday and July 4th. I could understand such pathological behavior on Independence Day. There is the heat of summer and outdoor parties with the omnipresence of alcohol and drugs. In such an environment, especially where alcohol and crack cocaine, methamphetamines, and other drugs are being consumed, there is an increased risk of arguments leading to aggressive behavior.

The composite of abusive behaviors becomes "the dark side of Easter".

For years I scheduled ride-outs with police officers on Easter Sunday. Each Easter Sunday I witnessed the same kind of celebrations with drinking and mean behavior.

At dusk when it is time for families to return home, things get ugly. Spouses argue about wanting to stay in conflict with the need to go home. Patience evaporates, and impatience is unleashed in verbal and aggressive language and action.

The following three stories have the common denominator described by the Apostle Paul as "darkness of evil."

Easter Sunday worship is over. The church is filled with regular worshipers plus the predictable Easter and Christmas Christians. My sermon described Mary Magdalene's experience at the tomb of the resurrected Jesus and its application to modernity. The sermon appeared to have touched some hearts. After the worship service and the traditional community lunch, the children, with Easter bunnies in tow, enjoy the annual Easter egg hunt. All is well on this Easter Sunday.

As is my tradition at mid-day on Easter Sundays, I dress in my Class B police chaplain's uniform (short sleeve, no tie) and drive to the police substation in my assigned sector. At show-up, Patrol Officer Bo and other patrol officers for the evening shift record instructions issued by the Shift Sergeant. They complete the shift's mandatory paperwork, then check out radios, radar guns, and shotguns. Bo and I exchange comments with other officers as we all proceed to parked police cruisers. Our shift begins at 3:30 Easter Sunday afternoon and will terminate at 1:30 Monday morning.

Stories Of The Street

The Risen Lord, Easter Baskets, and Filthy Wet Jeans

This particular Easter Sunday is a bright and sun-filled day. It is about four o'clock in the afternoon and we are on the way to the county jail with a very drunk homeless man in his late forties. We stop at a red light and are immediately flagged down by the car next to us.

Jennifer, the female driver, is in tears. A four-year-old girl is in the back seat appropriately buckled in her car seat. Jennifer's ex-husband Ron is in the passenger seat. They had decided to spend Easter Sunday together as a family for the benefit of their child.

Unfortunately, the day did not turn out as they'd hoped. Old personal issues surfaced and angry arguments followed. Still arguing, Jennifer is taking Ron back to his apartment. Because she is fed up with Ron, she stops us and insists that the officer remove Ron from her car. She is crying; the husband is crying; and the child is crying.

Jennifer releases the trunk lid from inside the car. The lid pops open, revealing a small bag filled with Ron's clothes. As he retrieves his bag, I could not help but notice several Easter baskets, stuffed bunnies, and Easter Sunday clothing for the mother and child. Since no crime has been committed or threat made, the officer has no reason to hold either the female driver or her distressed husband. The young, tearful, and frustrated man, with bag in hand, begins to walk dejectedly away in the direction of his apartment. Jennifer and her child drive away in the opposite direction toward Jennifer's apartment.

This is not the way this special day of the Risen Lord is supposed to end — sadness and loneliness, tears, and broken hearts.

Meantime Felix, the handcuffed homeless man in the back seat of our patrol car, is totally oblivious to the brokenness and sadness going on around him. He does not realize that he, too, is a part of the dark side of Easter.

We arrive at the jail and assist Felix inside the lockup. For the first time, I have a chance to really study him and see him as a person in the midst of evil and darkness that he might not understand.

Felix occupies the attention of the jailers through his obnoxious behavior. The zipper to his pants is open; his jeans are wet, filthy, and smell of urine. He is incapable of following jailers' orders and is led away by a young officer to be strip searched and dressed in jail clothing.

I wait at the pat-down desk as the police officer Bo completes his report. Felix, now dressed in orange prison overalls, is brought in the open collection area and disappears among the other prisoners. They will soon be relocated upstairs to jail cells.

Watching the collection of people in the gathering area, I notice Deputy Justin. He is the young jailer who led Felix away to change his filthy clothing. Justin walks to the desk and begins a conversation about the pitiful and harsh environment in which he works. Pointing his sterile-gloved hand toward the outside security door, he says; "I see a lot of bad stuff come through that door. The poor and drunk homeless guy, the wretched and cocaine-addicted street prostitute, the arrogant and belligerent college student on meth, the angry kid on crack – they all come through that door with handcuffs and an attitude."

With a sad and emotionally fatigued look on his face Justin says, "Chaplain, pray for me in my job of handling these misfits of society." This young jail officer (a public servant who is seldom if ever recognized or thanked by the community at large) is fully aware of what day it is and its meaning. Close to tears, the young man is overwhelmed by the dark side of Easter. Yet, he clearly knows about, and is yearning for, the Light that overcomes the darkness.

The Risen Lord, Easter Baskets, and Crack Cocaine

Stories Of The Street

A grandstand effect has been created as children and adults gather on multiple stairways and balconies of the apartment complex. The children all hold Easter baskets, stuffed bunnies, and other toys given to them on this Easter Sunday. It is a festive atmosphere as families celebrate the joyous day – except for the second floor balcony.

What these families are watching is not the joy of the day. They are witnessing the dark side of Easter. An angry man throws the belongings of an equally angry woman off the second-story balcony onto the courtyard of the housing complex. The characters of the drama are an HIV-positive man pimping for an angry prostitute.

Jesse, the pimp, is aggressive toward Rose, the prostitute. She is cheating him on his cut of her earnings. He sees the shortfall in his income as compromising his authority and the purchasing power to feed his crack cocaine addiction.

Someone in the gallery has called the police.

Walking into the courtyard of the apartment complex, Officer Bo and I are confronted by Jesse accusing Rose of being "unfaithful" to him, of sleeping with another man in the complex. He repeatedly calls her a whore. He is demanding Rose move out. On this Easter Sunday, he has started by throwing all her clothes over the second floor balcony to the amazement of the gathered families.

Later, Jesse tells us that he is a casualty of Hurricane Katrina and has moved to this area to escape the floodwaters in New Orleans. He met Rose and invited her to move into his apartment. She accepted.

Police Officer Terry, the back-up officer responding to the dispatch, listens to Rose's side of the story. Rose is angry and crying that she is being evicted by Jesse from their shared apartment. Between her tears, she claims she has nowhere to go. She denies any unfaithfulness to Jesse, saying that she had just been visiting with a friend in the apartment complex – an explanation that Jesse does not accept.

Rose shows no embarrassment about her underwear, multiple wigs, and muumuu dresses on display in the courtyard. She gathers the items up until her arms are filled while angrily cursing Jesse and his "unsportsmanlike conduct."

The scene is surreal. Easter baskets held by the children in the grandstands are as brightly colored as the scattered bras, panties, and wigs of the prostitute. The fragrant smoke rising silently from the family barbecue pits contrasts with the vulgar, loud belligerence of Jesse and Rose.

Both Bo and Terry know that there is more to this story than what Jesse and Rose are telling them. The two officers move off to the side, exchange information that they have gathered from Jesse and Rose. Then they return to the combatants. Slowly the truth begins to emerge from the inconsistencies of the two stories.

Jesse is a crack addict supporting his habit by pimping for Rose. Jesse saw Rose come out of an apartment where another male lives. He assumed she was working her profession without Jesse having made the arrangement. She is refusing to give Jesse his cut of her earnings thereby denying him another fix.

Contrary to Rose's statement that she has nowhere to go, she calls a friend who agrees to come by and pick her up. The friend soon arrives and Rose, dragging clothing and still cursing, passes through the walkway and leaves.

Because there was only a verbal confrontation, and because neither Jesse nor Rose struck each other, no arrest is made. A pat-down search of Jesse yields no illicit drugs or weapons on his person.

Bo, Terry, and I return to our patrol units, I turn and look at the young families and wonder what they are thinking. Was the Jesse/Rose incident an aberration on Easter Sunday? Or is it a reoccurring event in the daily life of the apartment complex where parents are struggling to raise their young children?

And what are the children thinking? Are they afraid such events will spill over and hurt them? Does the ugliness of this Easter Sunday forever shape an image contrary to the true meaning of Easter? Do they even know the true meaning of Easter?

Who is Easter Sunday for, anyway?

Is Easter only for the Christian families who go to church to sing and praise God? Or is Easter for the poor and perhaps hopeless people who live and raise their families only blocks away from the doorsteps of the church?

I suggest Easter is for both.

The Risen Lord, A Little Girl, Her Easter Bunny, and Screaming Violence

Within minutes following the Jesse and Rose incident we are dispatched to an apartment complex where domestic violence is occurring. The on-board computer describes the call as a WM (White male) being chased by a WF (White female) with a knife. The 911 call is from the cell phone of the victim as he outruns his alleged attacker.

Bo and I had both attended Easter services that morning at our respective churches. And here we are less than five hours later responding to a third act of domestic dysfunction.

Bo and I climb the stairs to the second story of the apartment complex and knock on the closed door of number 213 – the apartment number given the 911 operator by the caller. Following chaplain procedure, I stop midway up the stairs.

Gigi, age 26, answers the door. Immediately, in a loud and profane voice, she launches into a confession describing how she had slapped her boyfriend (Wade) six or seven times before chasing him around the apartment with a knife. The argument erupted because Wade was not actively seeking a job. Bo and I are amazed that Gigi is voluntarily giving a statement of aggression that would automatically lead to her arrest.

Gigi's beautiful blonde three-year-old daughter Kristen is also in the doorway, listening to the profanity and anger coming from her mother. Kristen, with her thumb in her mouth, is holding a new white Easter bunny with its ears lined in soft pink silk.

The fast-paced conversation continues with Gigi. Officer Terry, again the back-up officer to the dispatch, arrives and begins to climb the stairs to where we are standing. Terry turns around when a young man calls out to him. Wade, the purported victim, looks too youthful to be a part of this unfolding drama. He is clearly in over his head in his relationship with the more dominant and assertive Gigi. Terry turns and starts back down the steps to intercept and interview Wade.

Wade confirms Gigi's story about the argument with the exception that he claims she had chased him not only around the apartment with a knife, but subsequently down the steps and into the parking lot. He escaped by running into an adjacent open field and calling 911. He tells Officer Terry that he fears for his life.

Domestic violence calls are subject to specific laws that require officers to arrest a person if that person has hit or threatened another person. Clearly Gigi initiated her own arrest through her self-indicting statements made to Bo.

Officer Bo, knowing he is going to arrest Gigi, faces the dilemma of what to do with Kristen. Given the likelihood of Gigi becoming more aggressive than she already is, Bo asks Gigi to take Kristen back into the apartment. Kristen holds the white Easter bunny as her mother opens the door and nudges the little girl inside. Kristen is now alone in the apartment terrified about what is happening to her mother, and to herself.

As soon as Gigi closes the door, Bo tells her to turn around and put her hands behind her back. She does and Bo quickly handcuffs her. My mind is racing about what to do about the three-year-old little girl alone in the apartment.

Without any warning, Gigi turns violent. Screaming profanities, she goes after Bo kicking and head-butting. She furiously resists going down the steps to Bo's patrol unit. Other officers, responding to Bo's call for assistance, are now on the balcony and enter the fray to subdue Gigi.

The fight continues down the steps and into the parking lot. Officers struggle to get the screaming Gigi into the patrol car. Once inside the car she continues to fight. Kicking wildly at the windows of the car, she curses and spits at the police officers. It is an ugly scene.

At the top of the second floor balcony little Kristen has opened the apartment door. She is standing at the balcony guardrail, watching and listening to the violent scene in the parking lot below her. She begins to scream; "Mommy, Mommy!" with a passion so deep that it only could be uttered from a child's breaking heart.

I rush up the steps, pick Kristen up and go inside the apartment and try to distract her from the chaos. The white Easter bunny lies abandoned on the floor.

The interior of the apartment is totally empty except for a small TV, video player, and an air mattress. There are no appliances, no table in the kitchen, no bed or other furniture in the bedroom, and no clothes hanging in the closet. Rather, there is a pile of dirty clothing heaped on the floor in the bedroom closet. There are no resources in the apartment to support a "family" of three.

Because Gigi's violent and aggressive behavior inside the police cruiser continues, four officers pull her from the backseat, wrestle her to the pavement, and bind her feet with plastic ties. Face down on the pavement, immobilized by her bound hands and feet, Gigi is finally restrained.

Bo and Terry, being the officers first on the scene and responsible for the documenting the incident, turn their attention to Wade. All three men are on the balcony just outside the apartment door where I continue to try and distract Kristen – without much success.

The two officers review Wade's identification. They learn he is from North Carolina and that his parents were distraught about his attachment to Gigi. They tried desperately to convince Wade not to follow her to New Orleans. Against their will, Wade went with Gigi. Out of money and past due on multiple credit cards and apartment rents, the couple left New Orleans and migrated to Texas. Upon arrival in her hometown, Gigi retrieved Kristen from her hesitant mother and father.

In a sudden burst of passion, Wade erupts into a rescue mission to free Gigi. Bo and Terry slam him against the outside wall of the apartment. Gigi is screaming from the parking lot for Wade to save her. Wade is screaming at the police to let her go. Inside the apartment Kristen is crying desperately for her "Mommy". In the parking lot, on the balcony, and in the apartment, the pandemonium has exploded into three separate distinct partials — a screaming Gigi in the patrol car, a combative Wade in his dysfunctional attempt to save Gigi, and a terrified child screaming at the top of her little lungs.

I pick Kristen up, along with the white Easter bunny, and exit the apartment with my hand turning her head away from the scene. I take her down the long second-floor balcony to where a couple and a little boy Kristen's age are sitting. The couple is Hispanic and do not speak English. The mother offers Kristen an ice cream cone while smiling tenderly at the young girl. In the midst of the dark side of Easter this gentle mother is an angel reaching out to Kristen in a language of mercy that overrides the language of the tongue.

By this time the officers have learned the name of Gigi's mother and have called her to come get Kristen. Bo wants to avoid the child becoming a ward of Child Protective Services if at all possible. When Kristen's grandparents arrive, Kristen rushes to her grandmother in a scene of reunion. Clutching her Easter bunny with its pink-lined ears in her arms, she submerges herself into her grandmother's loving and unconditional embrace. For the first time on this Easter Sunday, little Kristen feels loved and secure.

The grandparents affirm they will be more focused on their efforts to legally adopt Kristen. It is clear that Kristen's grandmother fears for the little girl's safety. There is unspoken understanding between all of us that Gigi is not prepared to provide parental care for Kristen.

The now subdued Wade sits quietly against the outside wall of the apartment building. He tells me how he regrets not listening to his family in their pleas for him not to follow Gigi into uncharted waters. He is afraid to call them. He is embarrassed to go back.

Squatting next to him, I tell him that back in North Carolina his family probably still worries about him. That someone, if not all, in his family love him and are forgiving in their concern for his well-being. "Go back home. Go tell your parents you love them. Your family will embrace you as was the young man in the Bible who ventured off only to come back and be accepted, loved, and forgiven. They want you home Wade, and you need to be home. Go."

With tears in his eyes, he said; "Yes sir, I will."

Easter's Night

The end of the shift approaches. The sun that rose this morning giving hope and peace to all nations is now moving gently over the horizon, taking with it the Easter Story. In the darkness of the patrol car lighted only by the on-board computer screen, Bo and I are silent. Each of us contemplates, in the context of our own spiritual journey, the events of this Easter Sunday.

Our thoughts are interrupted by another dispatch to yet another family disturbance. A belligerent and aggressive man is in a rage and has assaulted his girlfriend, a mother of three. She called 911 for help, saying her boyfriend has shoved her into the living room wall.

We arrive and again find young children crying in fear of the angry man. As in all domestic disturbance calls, the aggressor is arrested. Bo takes the man outside, handcuffs him, and places him in the back seat of the patrol car.

Inside the unit, the man yells at us; "Hey man! This is Easter Sunday ain't it? I've been drinking! OK?"

6

"I Have Sinned"

Threats of suicide are not an infrequent call to police departments. Suicide threats must be met with an immediate and serious response. Fortunately, more often than not the calls are cries for help and do not actually result in a person's taking his or her own life. Nevertheless, there is a dysfunction somewhere in a person's life that stimulates suicidal thoughts.

On a Saturday afternoon Martha, a woman in her late forties, calls 911 to report her grown daughter Janie is distraught and threatening to take her own life. She asks that a police officer be sent to her apartment complex to prevent Janie from harming herself, and to give the parents time to locate Janie's husband Bobby. They also want to reach Janie's psychiatrist for assistance in getting her into a safe environment.

Janie had been alone in her apartment all morning. Her husband Bobby had gone to his downtown office to prepare for a major software presentation scheduled for Monday. During her time alone, Janie's thoughts turned to her own office environment and her attraction to a male officemate. The thoughts and urges she felt were in conflict with her moral values and her faith. Janie called her parents and they made a distress call to the police.

The 911 call from Janie's apartment came in at 1:37 p.m. Senior Patrol Officer (SPO) Rick and I arrive on scene at 1:45 p.m.

Janie's dad, Kenneth, flags us down in the parking lot of the apartment complex. He points to a ground level door and says his wife Martha is with Janie. His body language and tone of voice suggest disgust and irritation with his daughter. He tells us Janie has suffered from psychological problems since childhood. Failing to take her medicines always results in abnormal and depressive behavior.

Rick and I enter the apartment. Martha is sitting on the couch with a weeping and distraught Janie.

The mother explains that Janie wants a divorce from her husband because she has experienced desires for another man. Because lust is a violation of her Christian belief system, Janie feels a dissonance between faithfulness to her husband and her physical attraction to the young man in her office. Janie cannot justify the two extremes (physical faithfulness vs. imagined unfaithfulness). She sees no way out of her dilemma other than asking for a divorce to honor her desires; or to end her life.

Rick surveys the room and the intensity of the moment. In an effort to break the tension, he asks Janie's parents to "leave Janie alone with the Chaplain." He instructs Martha and Kenneth to come with him. Following standard police procedures, Rick will interview the parents on the circumstances surrounding Janie's distress.

Learning from Janie that her husband Bobby is at work downtown, Martha calls him on her cell phone to come home as quickly as possible.

I sit down on a footstool directly in front of Janie. My intent is to maximize one-on-one eye contact. I also want to be slightly below Janie's eye level to give her a sense of being in control.

It is immediately clear that Janie perceives herself as a sinful person. She feels a deep-seated guilt about the attraction she feels for her officemate. Janie tells me the man of her fantasies has no idea of her attraction to him.

Rev. Steve Best

We sit quietly while Janie speaks of her emotional and physical feelings for her office friend. As I listen to her, it is obvious that Janie is a scrupulous young woman. Her distress arises from her values and education being out of sync with her emotions.

I ask; "How do you view the Creation – as a pristine world of beauty and full of wonderment?"

Janie replies, "Yes."

"Do you admire and enjoy the beauty of creation?"

"Yes."

You know, to admire and enjoy creation is a wonderful gift from God. That includes admiring human beings as well as the environment with its entire splendor. To admire people, including one's self, is also to admire creation."

"Yes, lust will often enter into such admiration. When admiration and attraction preoccupy your thoughts, and they evolve into selfishness, then your admiration turns to lust."

"God is an understanding Creator. God created us to be attracted to the beauty of each other. When you let that attraction turn to lust, God offers you grace and forgiveness."

"Be honest about the love you feel for Bobby. Honesty is part of holistic healing; it will strengthen your marriage and your love for your husband. To give in to your feelings of guilt and betrayal will only add to your distress."

Janie nods in a tenuous, passive but positive response. She is quiet now, pensive, and prayerful.

> I pray: "Almighty God, to whom all hearts are open, all desires known, and from whom no secrets are hid: Cleanse the thoughts of our hearts by the inspiration of your Holy Spirit, that we may perfectly love you and worthily magnify your holy name, through Jesus Christ our Lord." [6]

---

[6] <u>Lutheran Book of Worship</u>, Augsburg Publishing House, Minneapolis, MN, 1979, p. 56

The door opens and Rick appears with Janie's husband Bobby.

Janie hurriedly gets up from the couch and rushes into Bobby's open arms. They hold each other in a long and loving embrace. Janie cries softly on Bobby's shoulder. He tells her how much he adores and loves her.

Bobby has known and loved Janie long enough to know that she is highly susceptible to extreme mood swings. Despite these mood swings, he loves her dearly.

Rick and I excuse ourselves from the room, leaving the two young people to work through the issues that brought Janie to an emotional flameout.

Outside, Janie's parents are appreciative. Martha talks about encouraging Janie to stay on her medications. She observed that when Janie feels good and all is well at home and at work, she stops taking her meds, not realizing the meds are a therapy, not a quick fix.

Kenneth says nothing except to shake our hands and thank us – his attitude seemingly more composed and accepting of Janie's emotional frailties.

For the moment, all is well.

7

Feathered Priorities

The cloud of dust and smoke several hundred yards in front of me tells me that I am approaching a serious automobile wreck on the highway.

A van is stopped in the northbound left lane of the highway with its left turn signal blinking. It was rear-ended by an approaching auto, sending the van scorching across the southbound lane and narrowly missing an oncoming pickup truck.

Pat is the driver of the southbound pickup. She immediately gets out of her vehicle and rushes to the rear-ended van imbedded in the roadside embankment. She assists the victim from the van and the two women sit down on the shoulder of the road. The injured accident victim, Monica, is resting in the arms of her rescuer. Someone has already called 911 and an ambulance is en route to the accident site.

Pat looks up at me. When I identify myself as a police chaplain, she smiles.

The stench of burnt rubber from the screeching tires still fills the air as the two try to make sense of what has just happened. Monica is screaming, "I have killed my baby!" I immediately go back to her abandoned vehicle to look for a child. The car is empty. There is no evidence of a child, nor is there a child car seat, baby clothes, diaper bag, or anything suggesting a child was or had been in the automobile.

Other drivers have stopped and are directing traffic around the scene. We are fixated on Monica and her repetitive crying out for her "baby."

I ask; "Where is your baby?"

She does not answer my question. She only cries out again "I've killed my baby!".

I ask again; "Where is your baby?"

This time, Monica holds up a white cloth about the size of a man's handkerchief. She opens the crumbled cloth and exposes two small baby birds. One is dead, the other is alive. Focusing her eyes on the dead bird, Monica repeats her bursts of despair; "I have killed my baby!" We all look at each other in disbelief, including Pat, the woman driver gingerly holding Monica.

Astonished, no one says anything.

I ask Monica; "Are you married?"

"Yes."

"What is your husband's name and phone number?"

"Keith," she answers, and gives me his number.

Using my cell phone, I call Keith's office, explaining to the operator that the call is an emergency call for Keith. I am passed through to his office. I explain to Keith that Monica has been in a serious accident, but she appears to be OK. I tell him an ambulance is on the way and that he should stay in his office until an Emergency Medical Services (EMS) team arrives. "They will determine what hospital your wife will be taken to. I will call you back as soon as I know."

Keith's immediate response is not what I expected. He totally ignores the well-being of Monica and her medical and mental condition. Instead Keith asks; "How are the birds? Where are they?"

"One is dead; the other appears to be OK."

"Where will the birds go?"

"I don't know, but I will find out and call you when I know to which hospital Monica is being transported."

The EMS unit arrives at the same time as sheriff deputies and a Texas Department of Public Safety (DPS) trooper. The officers immediately begin to secure the accident scene, direct traffic, and start their standard witness interviews and accident investigation procedures.

EMS personnel check Monica's vital signs and look for any spinal or neurological injury. They determine she does need medial attention and announce Monica will be taken to a major trauma center. In a panic Monica asks, "What about my baby?" EMS personnel look at each other in total surprise as Pat takes the crumbled cloth out of Monica's hand and shows its contents to them. They shake their heads in disbelief.

Carefully EMS personnel place Monica on a gurney and secure her with multiple straps. Leveling the gurney as they pick it up, they load her into their waiting EMS unit and leave for the distant trauma hospital with strobe lights and siren running Code 3.

The designated hospital is not far from Keith's office. I call him back with the information that his wife will be at the hospital within 30 to 40 minutes. I tell him how to access the emergency room at the large hospital and that he should be there when Monica arrives. Ignoring my suggestions, Keith again asks; "Where are the birds going?" I tell him a deputy sheriff is taking them to the county sheriff's office. He proclaims in a hurried voice; "I am on the way!" – meaning to the sheriff's office.

I pushed the "end" button of my cell phone and thought about what Keith had just said. My reaction to his words is; "You jerk! You will actually pass the ambulance carrying your wife to the ER while you are going in the opposite direction to retrieve two birds, one of which is dead!"

Later I would learn that there is an active black market for Central and South American birds and their chicks. This could well be the driving force behind Keith's and Monica's pathological concerns for the two birds.

Pat and I prepare to leave the scene. We embrace each other as if to say; "Well-done, friend; I am glad we were here." I ask if she is OK; she says she is fine. We hug, and I turn and go to my car.

Driving slowly toward home, I begin to reflect on the events of the past hour as the serious and strange drama unfolded. The distorted image of two little crumpled birds wrapped in a handkerchief and serving the materialistic priorities of Monica and Keith did not, to me, reflect God's vision of creation.

Rev. Steve Best

8

The Devil Is in the Details

Standing between two police officers, the middle-aged man exclaimed, "I thought I had finally won something…I thought I had come upon a blessing."

That was the explanation of an elected school board trustee named Bernie, age 42. He first tried to cash a $2,300 check the day before. Because the check was drawn on a bank located on the East Coast, the store manager asked Bernie to come back the next day. Confirming her suspicions, she discovered the check was drawn on a non-existent bank. The manager told her staff that when Bernie returned to the store that they should stall him while she summoned the police.

The next morning Bernie did return to the check-cashing store and the manager's instructions were immediately put into action.

Dispatch, while communicating with the store manager, radioed our patrol car that a male with short hair and facial hair, wearing cutoffs and red T-shirt, was attempting to cash a counterfeit check. Running Code 2 (overhead lights without siren), the officer I am riding with that morning points out a man matching Bernie's description. He is walking down the sidewalk of the strip center. He does not appear to be in a hurry as he walks in a direction away from the check-cashing store and toward a convenience store.

The officer stops Bernie who appears totally surprised. The officer asks him if he had just tried to cash a check next door. "Yes, sir," he responds politely.

"Did you know the check was counterfeit?"

"Of course not. Why would I try to cash a check that is no good?"

"Do you have ID on you?"

"Yes sir."

"Let me see it, please."

The suspect's driver license displays his name as Bernie, date of birth, address, height, color of eyes, and gender.

The officer points at a red pick-up truck parked in between the check-cashing store and the convenience store and asks, "Is that your truck?"

Bernie replies, "Yes, sir."

The officer radios the personal data as well as the truck's license number to dispatch. Dispatch responds within minutes, saying that the truck is not reported stolen. However, the officer's computer screen communicates that Bernie has a previous arrest record for assault.

Exiting the patrol car, the officer asks Bernie: "Do you have any outstanding warrants"

Bernie: "No sir.

Officer: "Have you ever been arrested before?"

Bernie: "Yes sir"

"What for?"

"I was arrested for assault last year. My wife and me were fighting and I hit her. She called the police and I was arrested."

Following police procedures, the officer handcuffs Bernie, nods his head in the direction of the check-cashing store and says to Bernie; "Come with me, please."

We start back toward the check-cashing store, passing Bernie's truck on the way. The bed of the truck is loaded with sports equipment and ice chests filled with perishable food and drinks. Lying on the passenger side seat and floorboard are school board manuals and other supporting documentation. Bernie explains he is a school board member and a director of a summer youth sports league.

Reaching the store, both the cashier and the manager verify Bernie is the person who tried to cash the fraudulent check. They confirm that they instructed Bernie the day before to come back the next day.

This is the way the scam worked: Bernie received in the mail a $2,300 check and a letter stating that he had won a $1,555 lottery prize. The letter instructed the victim to cash the $2,300 check and send the entire amount back by Western Union. The lottery would send him another check for $1,555.

"I thought I had finally won something…I thought I had come upon a blessing."

Several months earlier Bernie was elected to his first term as a board member for an independent school district. He is also a founder and the director of an area youth sports organization to which he was on his way when he stopped to cash the check. Given his background as a responsible decision-maker for a school board and a director of a youth organization, it seemed out of character that a community leader like Bernie would fall for such an obvious scam. He did, out of greed. And it cost him dearly.

Although Bernie seems honest and forthright in his explanation to cash the check, his story simply did not make sense. He explained he had taken his wife to work, and then stopped by the check-cashing store to collect on the lottery check. He claimed the check-cashing stop was on the way to the youth athletic fields. However, in order for Bernie to accomplish all three tasks as stated, he would have had to drive across the city twice. The expenditure of time and resources to accommodate the desire to collect unearned money simply could not be interpreted as naiveté.

Inside the store the officer tells the handcuffed Bernie that he is under arrest for forgery by attempting to cash a counterfeit check. Bernie, looking panicky and agitated, retorts in a loud voice: "You think I'd risk everything I've worked for, for just $2,300? Man, I've worked too hard to deserve this."

During the conversations between the first responding officer and the check-cashing store manager, and between Bernie and the officer, a back-up officer arrives at the scene. The back-up officer listens to both sets of conversations, asking a few questions during the sorting out of facts.

Bernie is placed in the rear seat of a patrol car. The two police officers begin to decide whether they should arrest him for attempted fraud, or let him go. One officer is sympathetic toward Bernie. Yes, Bernie believed he indeed had won some form of a lottery – and, yes, Bernie should have known better, but the lure of money overrode his good judgment.

The other officer takes the position that Bernie, as a community leader, is intelligent enough not to fall victim to such an obvious scam. The officer is firm in his conviction that Bernie was attempting to cash a worthless check over $200, which is a felony. Given his prior arrest record, the officer holds the position that Bernie should be arrested and booked for intent to defraud.

The second officer prevails, and Bernie is arrested and booked into county jail.

Bernie's loaded truck was impounded with my request to the wrecker driver that all the perishable food items be placed under refrigeration. He promised it would be.

What would be the results of Bernie's arrest in terms of his career and leadership positions in the community? Would he be dismissed from the school board? Would he be fired as the director of a youth sports organization? How did Bernie's prior police record influence the officers' decision to arrest him, or did it?

A review of the school board minutes shows that Bernie remained on the board from the time of his arrest through the time his board term expired. He missed only two board meetings during the 11-month period.

Rev. Steve Best

All during the conversations with the two police officers, Bernie never accused or implied racial discrimination by the two arresting police officers.

The discussion between the two officers to arrest Bernie, or let him go, illustrates a continuing difficulty for police. Most people law enforcement officers encounter on a daily basis tend to lie to them. Listening to lies creates doubt and suspicion in all conversations. At some point in each encounter a decision must be made to believe or not believe, to arrest or not to arrest.

Even though criminal and civil laws and police policies clearly delineate the rules of the game, there remain gray areas on the street. The devil is in the details of this story, and the two responding officers had to sort through abstractions and facts, between judgment and behavior.

In the end the officer arguing for the letter of the law prevailed over the abstract analysis of Bernie's character and honesty.

Street Images II
God's Hand Stories

"When I consider the heavens …
the work of thy fingers"

Psalm 8

9

When Bad Things Happen

The evening shift "show-up" is complete and Patrol Officer Craig and I transfer our gear from our personal vehicles to the patrol unit. We drive out of the substation parking lot on schedule and head toward our assigned district within the area command sector. It is just after five in the afternoon.

The January sun is bright as it begins its descent into the western horizon. The north wind is gusty and cold. The radio dispatchers are busy assigning officers to a variety of non-critical calls. But that changes with a command to "be on the lookout" (BOLO) for a specific vehicle possibly involved in a murder in another sector of the city. Craig enters the across-town sector's computer identification code and receives a responding computer screen reporting two sisters had discovered the body of their older sister when they returned home from school.

Since the crime scene does not involve our sector, we were not dispatched to the crime scene. Craig makes note of the vehicle description and we comment briefly on an apparent tragedy unfolding across town.

Suddenly the radio erupts with a flurry of radio traffic by dispatch and officers responding to a bank robbery only blocks away from our location. We are instructed to set up at a given intersection to direct vehicular and pedestrian traffic away from the armed robbery scene.

Thus begins several hours of standing in the cold winter wind while crime scene investigators gather the data and physical evidence from the targeted bank. The afternoon fades into evening and the cold, blustery wind seems to increase in intensity. Traffic is minimal, making the time pass slowly, so we stay close to the patrol unit to draw warmth from its idling engine and to take brief respites inside the warm vehicle.

It is during one of the respites that Craig's cell phone rings. He responds to the caller in a series of "Yes, sirs," writes down an address on his note pad, and concludes the one-sided conversation with a final "Yes, sir." Quickly he drops his idling patrol unit into gear, turns to me and says, "That was my Sergeant. You are being called to the murder scene of the teenager. They need you to help with the family."

The 20-minute trip across town gives me time to calm my anxiety to the call-out. I pray that I will have the wisdom to help the family find something to sustain them in their confrontation with tragedy. I have no idea what to expect – no idea of what I was getting into as we near the scene. The advice given by one of my seminary professors resounded repeatedly in my head: "Remember – YOU are the God person in the room" when caring for a family confronted with end-of-life circumstances.

It is dark as we pull up to the scene. Red, blue, and white strobe lights from emergency vehicles fill the darkness. Officers have barricaded the street of the family home. Craig radios the officer-in-charge that we are on scene. We learn the family is no longer at the residence. They have been transported to police headquarters downtown for questioning.

The night seems darker and colder as we drive to the downtown police headquarters building. Neither of us speak. We are both lost in our own thoughts of the horror for the young girl and her family at an hour when other families are going about their daily routines. Television news coverage of a vicious rape and murder of a college student in a middle-class neighborhood will soon disrupt those routines.

The victim is 19-year-old Lisa. She is a college student. She has two younger sisters; one in high school, the youngest one in middle school.

Lisa had returned home from school around 3:00 p.m. and finds her mother's bedroom in disarray. The dresser drawers are open. Clothing is strewn on the floor along with her mother's empty jewelry box. Lisa picked up the bedroom phone and called her dad. She told him that something was wrong and that she was scared. He was telling her to get out of the house when the line went dead. The intruder had cut the line as Lisa was calling for help.

Without thinking to call 911, Lisa's dad Robert began to race home only to become mired in late afternoon traffic. He is frustrated in not being able to speed to his daughter's frightened call.

We are told by officers at the scene that the two younger sisters returned home from school about 4:30 p.m. Lisa's car was not parked along side the curb as it normally was when she got home first. The back door was unlocked and upon entering the house they sensed something was wrong. The house was too quiet

The older of the two girls walked down the hallway to Lisa's room and is horrified with what she sees. Lisa was lying on her bed with a knife protruding from her chest. Her clothes had been torn off her. Her hands are tied and her mouth is taped.

The 16-year-old sister used her cell phone to call 911 to report Lisa had been stabbed. In an act of courage and compassion, the high school aged sister grabbed her younger sister to keep her from seeing Lisa's mutilated and nude body. They ran out of the house in fear of their lives. Their 911 call was the origin of the city-wide BOLO Officer Craig and I heard earlier in the shift.

Lisa's mother was at a doctor's office and had no idea of what was happening to her family until she arrived home to see police cars, crime scene vehicles, ambulances, and the predictable crowd that gathers around all crime scenes.

Homicide detectives quickly transport the family to police headquarters to gather relevant information. They are interested in all primary and secondary family members' backgrounds; names of the victim's friends including boyfriends, work associates, and classmates that might possibly have a reason to do Lisa harm. They are also interested in recent events leading up to the murder.

At police headquarters the emotions are far too raw for the family to get past the question of "Why?" It is far too early to ask; "What do we do now that it has happened?" Instead we have a moment-to-moment survival scene for the family which is enveloped in the gruesome murder of their beloved daughter and sister. At a time like this it feels as if God's mercy and compassion have disappeared. But a remnant of faith reminds us that somehow God's *presence* is near.

I climb the stairs leading to the mezzanine floor of police headquarters. The family, with the exception of the father, is gathered in a reception area. Lisa's mother is seated, head down, hands folded in her lap, and crying softly. Seated next to her is her 12-year-old daughter, Lisa's baby sister. Fear, confusion, and grief are clearly visible on her young face.

The 16-year-old stands some distance from her mother and sister. Her eyes stare into space, her face expressionless. It is apparent she is internalizing the horrific sight of her dead sister.

I approach the mother and kneel down in front of her, placing my hands over hers.

"I am so sorry this has happened to Lisa and to your family."

She acknowledges my presence with a nod. Talking in an almost inaudible voice, she describes the loving relationship she had with Lisa. She is crying, her head down, her shoulders swaying slightly. Tears roll down her cheeks and fall silently onto her blouse.

Gently I say:

Lord God, we cry out to you for help in our despair. Hold Lisa in your grace. Accept her into your kingdom; give her peace from the violent acts committed against her. Love her, and give this family the courage to stand against this violent assault that claims the life of Lisa and penetrates our souls with a deepening loss.

We remain in the "valley of the shadow of death" for several minutes.

A homicide detective exits an interview room, walks over to me and asks that I go visit with Lisa's father. Nodding his head to his left, he gestures to the interview room a short distance away.

The walls of the small interview room are covered in soundproof material resembling cardboard egg cartons. A rectangular government-issue metal table is against the wall with two stiff back chairs – one at the end of the table, the other alongside the table, giving an interviewer more space to take notes. A small camera is mounted in a corner of the ceiling. It looks down on the sterile scene, silently listening and recording the scene.

Robert is seated at the end of the table facing the door. He is angry and frustrated. He slams his fist repeatedly into his open palm as he places blame on himself for not reaching home in time to save Lisa. He talks of Lisa being born in Europe and moving to the United States with her family a year and a half before her death.

Robert is in tears. He is remorseful when he describes Lisa as his "little girl, a daddy's girl." He moves his head from side to side in denial that she is dead.

We talk for 40 minutes about his life's journey and his love for his wife and his children. When the conversation becomes repetitive, I interrupt him and ask if he would like a prayer before we return to his family. He readily agrees.

Trying to block the ever-present eyes of the ceiling camera and the certainty of a hidden microphone, I move from my

Rev. Steve Best

chair to his side in the hope of achieving some level of privacy. I place my hands over his clenched fist:

> Father God, we lift up to you the soul of Robert's beloved Lisa. Receive her, O Lord, into your kingdom. Be kind and gracious to her, giving her an eternal peace that only you can give. Help Lisa's family and assure them of your love and the courage to accept the reality of a tragedy we cannot understand. Help us to be aware not only of the dark shadows of death, but also of the bright splendor of life eternal. Help the family face their life with strength; and give them the grace and your reassuring presence to go on. Comfort them and uphold them in their hour of darkness. In Jesus' name, we pray. Amen.

I keep my hands over Robert's fist to indicate I want him to remain quiet. Looking straight into his eyes, I remind him he is the leader of his family. He needs to be the strong one in the family, that he must provide courage for his grieving wife and daughters. He nods his head and we stand to leave the room and return to the reception area.

In concern for the young victim's family we are reminded of Billy Graham's statement:

> Whatever the circumstances, whatever the call, whatever the duty, whatever the price, whatever the sacrifice – His strength will be your strength in your hour of need. [7]

---

[7] <u>Peace With God: The Secret of Happiness</u> – Billy Graham, W Publishing Group, 1984, p. 271

10

An Angel Appears

I open the interview room door and motion for Robert to lead the way to his family and friends clustered a short distance away. When we approach the grieving family, I notice a young woman in her thirties, a work associate of Lisa's mother. She seems to glide as she approaches the mother, bends down and embraces her with the tenderness of a guardian angel. The angel's voice is soft as she speaks to the mother in tones of compassion and love. She embraces the 12-year-old and the three women are silent as they search for meaning in the midst of their despair.

The angel rises and moves to Lisa's 16-year-old sister standing alone some distance away. Her back is to the gathering group of friends. A quiet conversation ensues as the angel stands with her arm around the waist of the soulful and withdrawn teenager. The angel is clearly comforting the teenager, affirming that God "will raise (her) up on eagle's wings, bear (her) on the breath of dawn,

Rev. Steve Best

make (her) to shine like the sun, and hold (her) in the palm of his hand." [8]

Hours pass. Some of Lisa's friends arrive, including Lisa's boyfriend. Awkward silence prevails as young women cry and young men stare into space, lost in their anger and sadness that someone would commit such a vicious crime against their friend Lisa.

The wall clock shows that it is now after 9:00 p.m. Victim Services personnel have arrived and in their professional manner begin caring for the family. They write down the names of additional family members and close friends who need to be called with the death notification. They ask what clothing and toiletries the family needs for several days away from home. They reassure the family that Lisa's body has been removed from the house and is being treated with respect. Lisa's mother says she cannot stay in their house that night, nor does she ever want to return to it.

A detective emerges from his office and asks if anyone knows the name "Billy Ray." Several of the gathered youth respond in unison, "He works with Lisa at a restaurant in the shopping center." In unison they nod their heads in a visionary direction. The detective listens closely to the young people, takes copious notes, turns abruptly toward his office and disappears behind a hallway door.

Billy Ray had called the police department when he saw the television news of Lisa's death. When pressed about his interest in the case, he became agitated and hung up. During an interview with his employer, police learned where Billy Ray lived and proceeded to a nearby apartment complex. Inside his apartment they found jewelry matching the description of the items missing from Lisa's family home. He had also stolen Lisa's car which was the origin of the citywide BOLO alert.

---

[8] With One Voice, Augsburg Fortress, Minneapolis, MN, 1995, Hymn #779 - On Eagle's Wings, Text and Music: Michael Joncas, b. 1951, edited to 3rd person

The Victim Services people make reservations at a local hotel for the family to stay overnight and probably for several days thereafter. There will be no charge to the family. Victim Services personnel will stay with the family until they indicate they are ready to retire for the night.

Family and friends pair off and hold on to each other as they begin their way down the mezzanine steps to street level. Along the way I turn around and see the angelic young woman standing on the top step of the mezzanine level. She has a gentle smile on her radiant face as if she is offering a blessing of love to Lisa's mother and siblings. When the group reaches the street level I turn and look again. The angel has disappeared.

Craig, who had transported me first to the murder scene and then to police headquarters, stayed with me the entire evening. He told me later that this was his first experience with the murder of a young person. He wanted to see how families react to tragedy. He wanted to learn how he could best serve another family under similar circumstances.

Even though Craig was not in the interview room with Lisa's dad and me, he stayed near Lisa's mother and her two teenage daughters throughout the evening. Providing a sense of security for them, he was attentive and sensitive to family and friends' reaction to the tragedy.

Craig also witnessed first-hand the contributions that victim services personnel rendered to those mourning the loss of Lisa. No doubt he has since worked other tragedies and has used the lessons of that cold January night we shared.

The next day Billy Ray was arrested and charged with capital murder in the stabbing death of Lisa. Under state law, he could have faced the death penalty.

Instead, the federal district court judge agreed to a plea bargain of consecutive sentences of life in prison followed by 20 years for felony burglary with a deadly weapon.

Robert was not as willing to negotiate Billy Ray's fate. He was bitter and publicly called Billy Ray a coward who did not have the courage to challenge Lisa's boyfriend for Lisa's attention. He clearly wanted the state to execute the killer of his beloved Lisa.

The "angel" that appeared in this story of a young woman's murder brought compassion, grace, care-giving and care-receiving, touching and holding, and, just maybe, forgiveness.

Our emotions dictate our capability to forgive, or to hate and seek retribution for those who wrong us. For Robert, a hateful vengeance toward Billy Ray was a primal response to the premeditated rape and brutal murder of his beloved daughter.

The never-ending flow of broadcast and print media coverage of violent crimes often reports that victims and victims' families are filled with the level of vengeance demonstrated by Robert. However, there are also stories in which victims and victim's families offer reconciliation and forgiveness to the perpetrator of a crime against them.

Which of the two responses (vengeance or forgiveness) is the more appropriate for victims of violent crime within the Biblical writings of *an eye for an eye, a tooth for a tooth* in contrast to *love one another as I have loved you?*

To forgive a perpetrator of a vicious and deeply personal crime against a person or a family member is grace, not retribution. However, such a virtue may also mask and repress emotions of anger and revenge resulting in a "forgiveness and love whose effects are not reconciliation and new life, but rather repressed bitterness and hatred." [9]

In her autobiography, The Hiding Place, Corrie Ten Boom tells about her capture and detention in a Nazi concentration camp. She describes in detail her malnutrition,

---

[9] Embodying Forgiveness – A Theological Analysis – L. Gregory Jones, William B Eerdmans Publishing Company, Grand Rapids, Michigan, 1995, p. 245

the mistreatment by the guards, the death of her sister. But she also emphasizes her undying faith in God throughout her imprisonment.

Following her liberation, she committed her life to the church. She became a sought-after spokesperson on the grace of God in cruel and humiliating circumstances.

In every speech she made, she tells her story. She talks of forgiveness of those who perpetrated horrific hardships on her and her sister. She is not hesitant to expound on the scenes of naked Jewish women being mocked by German guards and officials. She remembers clearly the heaps of clothing that once covered them and now lay on the ground as remnants of Jewish society, gassed en masse, and buried en masse. She becomes solemn as she tells of her sister's blanched face before she finally died from the abuse.

Anger and vengeful thoughts boiled within Corrie Ten Boom for years as she grieved over her sister's death and the innumerable deaths of others at the hands of evil.

The emotions of repressed bitterness and hatred were always just under the surface until one day when she was speaking to a large congregation and saw in the audience the guard who had abused her so badly. Following her talk, he came up to her and greeted her with a warm smile and open hand. She described how her hand would not move from her side to shake his outstretched hand, how she could not speak – her throat literally closing down. Her entire body froze in old fears and hatred.

At that moment she saw the guard in the light of Christ as a child of God. She opened her hand, smiled, and greeted him. All the hatred she had carried all those years simply left her, and she forgave him in a gesture of authentic virtue.

Corrie Ten Boom's initial frozen reaction was natural. Her ability to overcome her anger and fear and to shake the guard's hand can only be described as divine mediation.

If someone causes suffering or death for an individual, the victim's family and friends as well as the community at large demand that the criminal suffer as well. Punishment for the perpetrator seems to ease the pain of the community and its victimized citizens. Under the rule of law, we administer punishment under the banner of criminal justice.

There are many, many people who hold to the view of cause and effect. They believe the world is held in the grip of a vengeful God. Ironically, they hold such a view because they believe in justice. Thus, at times of personal difficulty and suffering, people still say with genuine bewilderment, "I don't know what I've done to deserve this." This form of thinking is called the Doctrine of Retribution.

Like Corrie Ten Boom when confronted by her Nazi guard, Robert now faces a head-on life and death struggle of retribution vs. redemption. And, like Corrie Ten Boom, Robert will probably struggle for years to move from retribution to redemption. And, there is no guarantee he will ever reach the redemption side of the equation and be able to extend his hand to Billy Ray in genuine forgiveness.

Eventually Corrie Ten Boom reached reconciliation that expunged her hatred for her personal enemy and moved toward a genuine gesture of authentic virtue. It was not easy, but her spiritual maturation enabled her to do so. She writes: "When He tells us to love our enemies, He gives, along with the command, the love itself." [10]

At some point along his life's journey, I pray that Robert will achieve a genuine measure of forgiveness toward Billy Ray. Right now, his feelings are too raw and the loss too great for him to see beyond his grief, anger, and desire for retribution.

Quoting L. Gregory Jones:

> Throughout the craft of forgiveness, and in our practice of loving enemies, we are involved in learning to become holy through seeking to heal

---

[10] <u>The Hiding Place</u> – Corrie Ten Boom with John and Elizabeth Sherrill, Barbour Publishing, Inc., Uhrichville, Ohio, 1971, p.231

broken relations. Given the persistence of sin and evil in our midst, that often involves difficult discernment in the power of the Spirit. However, it also compels us to ask one final question: Are there some people, who – at least in this life and in this world – are unforgivable? In the final analysis, what kind of story should we tell? [11]

---

[11] Embodying Forgiveness – A Theological Analysis – L. Gregory Jones, William B. Eerdmans Publishing Company, Grand Rapids, Michigan, 1995, pp. 277-278.

11

Gooseneck Trailers and Grace

"Nora 503."

Nora is a sector of the city with specified boundaries. Within the sector are multiple districts. Each district has at least one officer assigned to it based on the call history of that district.

"Nora 503. Go ahead," replies Officer Brandon.

"Minor traffic accident 5000 block of Raleigh involving a large trailer and a small car. Occupant of the small car is reported to be angry and aggressive. Participants are in parking lot of Wal-Mart."

Brandon responds; "10-4," acknowledging the message.

Immediately focusing his attention on his on-board computer, Brandon keys up the waiting call. The computer screen displays details of the reported accident. "Traffic incident in 5000 block Raleigh – female driver of small vehicle – aggressive toward male driver of a pickup with trailer. Location – Wal-Mart parking lot, NE corner of intersection with Glover Blvd." We are traveling to the scene in Code One – no activated overhead lights and no siren. This call is not an emergency.

Stories Of The Street

As we pull into the parking lot, a frantic young man runs to our patrol unit. Jeff is profusely apologizing for the accident. He is driving a new Dodge 3500 Series Dually four-axial truck. He is pulling a 24-foot, six-axial aluminum-paneled livestock trailer. Together the truck and gooseneck trailer represent an investment of at least $60,000.

The name "gooseneck" comes from the tongue of the trailer reaching over the rear of a "dually" or pickup truck and linked to a plated ball-hitch bolted to the reinforced bed of the truck. The hitch is directly over the truck's rear axial enabling a truck to carry a much heavier load than the traditional bumper-ball hitch trailers. Its structure resembles the neck of a goose – hence its name, "gooseneck" trailer.

Jeff is from South Texas, on his way to the Texas Panhandle. He is driving alone on his long journey.

Off to the left side of the truck and trailer and standing next to a small dark sedan is a woman shouting profanities at Jeff. Monica has an angry assessment of Jeff's ability to drive his truck and trailer: "He doesn't know how to drive that thing!"

Inside Monica's car are three small children ages three, four, and five. All are wearing seatbelts.

The children are frightened not only by the accident, but by the aggressive reaction of their mother toward Jeff and the police officers. Looking up at the huge trailer, Monica and her children must have thought that a mountain was descending upon them. The sound of crunching metal and plastic pulling off the front end of their small car only added to the frightening experience. Fortunately there were no injuries to the children or Monica in this slow-moving incident.

The incident began as Monica was leaving the Wal-Mart parking lot at the same moment that Jeff was entering the lot and initiating a turn into a parking lot lane with its arrows pointing toward the store. He did not give the long trailer sufficient space to negotiate the turn and it "cut the corner" across the front of Monica's small vehicle. The moving trailer removed the grillwork, lights, bumper and most of the left front fender.

As both parties approach us, Officer Brandon separates the two, asking Monica to return and wait in her car while he takes a statement from Jeff. Because of Monica's anger, it takes a few minutes for Brandon to convince her to return to her car. During those few minutes Jeff, literally shaking from apprehensiveness of what could happen to him, recognizes that I am a chaplain and rushes toward me, beseeching me to pray with him. Caught completely off guard by his rush to prayer in such a minor incident, and before I can formulate what to pray for, Jeff goes into a rambling and fast-moving "O Jesus" prayer. Sadly, the prayer is totally focused on himself with no reference to the safety and well-being of the victims of his carelessness. It is all about Jeff.

Because the accident occurred on private property, police are not required to issue tickets for traffic violations. Instead, an officer will give each participant a "blue form" to complete and file with their respective insurance companies.

Not realizing what is going on at curbside, Brandon inadvertently interrupts Jeff's fast moving prayer. He calls Jeff over to the truck and trailer. Brandon hands a set of blue forms to Jeff with instructions on how to complete the documentation of the accident. Monica has already been briefed on the process and is busy completing her set of documents.

While Brandon and Jeff are engaged in conversation of the accident, I walk over to Monica. She has calmed down and we visit over the issues of safety for her children. I compliment her for having all three children seat-belted. She tells me the source of her anger is the result of being a single mom and working long hours to make ends meet. Her fatigue after a long day simply overpowered her business-like demeanor and she "blew up at the young man who obviously did not know how to drive his truck". In her calmness, she talks about how to get her car repaired and the serious issue of transportation for her and her children.

Jeff completes his forms and gives them to Officer Brandon to exchange with Monica. The officer purposely keeps the two separated and distributes the completed forms without either party having access or conversation with the other.

Jeff is free to go. He climbs into his truck, starts the diesel engine, drops the big rig into gear and begins to move forward. We all watch as he pulls away from the scene. We watch him begin his turn toward the store's main entrance. Again he does not allow the gooseneck trailer ample room to clear parked cars. In absolute astonishment we see and hear him take off the entire rear bumper and rear panels of an unattended Honda Accord. Jeff had not gone 20 feet before he hit the Honda. In disbelief Jeff jumps from his truck, and in tears he screams apologies to anyone who will listen.

Brandon, the Wal-Mart security guard, and I stand in awe of what just happened.

With a straight face Brandon looks at Jeff and says; "Here is another blue form."

The second collision catapults Monica out of her wrecked sedan. Fortunately she stays next to her car and does not attempt to charge toward Jeff. That doesn't mean she remains quiet.

Monica is screaming, at the top of her lungs, "I told you he couldn't drive that thing! Look at what he has done now! I told you so."

It was all that Brandon and I could do to keep from laughing at this comedy of errors occurring right in front of us. Obviously, we could not laugh until we left the scene some time later.

Jeff's hands and shoulders are trembling as he begins to fill out the second set of forms on the sideboards of his now battle-tested gooseneck trailer. Although I cannot see his face from where I stand, it appears that Jeff's emotions have taken over his countenance and, by the shaking of his shoulders, I can tell he is in tears.

Moments later a young woman emerges from the Wal-Mart store and approaches the surreal scene. She is dressed in business casual clothing, professional in her demeanor with a posture of self-assurance. Lori presents herself as a well-mannered young woman.

Lori looks astonished at the rear bumper of her new Honda Accord lying on the ground and the crushed tail lights and rear quarter panels dangling from the car's frame. She looks to the police officer and calmly asks; "What happened to my car?" Before Brandon can respond, Jeff falls on his knees in front of her and begins a litany of desperate apologies. You could see the fear on his face, thinking that Lori, too, would verbally attack him in his disgrace.

Lori smiles at Jeff and says; "Oh, that's OK; these things happen."

Brandon, the Wal-Mart security guard, and I are amazed at Lori's reaction. It is in stark contrast to Monica's reaction. Both women were vehicular victims initiated by the same accident-prone offender, but their responses were 180 degrees different.

Monica and Lori illustrate that not all stories in this book tell of traumatic experiences that play heavily on the hearts and minds of police officers. There are incidents where officers find space to diplomatically appreciate the Abbott and Costello qualities of a situation.

My first thought is to honor the grace of Lori's forgiving spirit toward Jeff. After all, her recent model car would be much more costly to repair than Monica's car.

But, I also see the faces of Monica's three frightened young children, and I remember her statement about being a single mom working two jobs to make ends meet. These things make me more understanding of her aggressive reaction to the situation.

Brandon lifts the radio mike from its dashboard mount; "Nora 503."

"Go ahead," responds the dispatcher.

"10-50 – Wal-Mart parking lot – south side." (Request for wreckers)

"10-4."

Monica and Lori have both called relatives to pick them up. They arrive in a short time and the two women leave the scene.

Police policy requires police officers to stay at an accident scene until the scene is cleared of all wreckage and of anyone involved in an incident. Waiting for a wrecker service to pick up Monica's and Lori's vehicles, we watch Jeff put his large truck in gear and move forward with its long gooseneck trailer in tow. He has reentered the marked aisle of the parking lot and is driving toward the front entrance to the store. We look at each other knowing full well that he is going to find a very short turning radius when he reaches the end of the access lane.

Patrolman Brandon and I prepare to leave the Wal-Mart parking lot, smiling at each other and hoping we do not receive another dispatch to 5000 block of Raleigh – Wal-Mart parking lot. We drive off with Brandon radioing "Code 4" to headquarters (available for next call).

Gooseneck trailers and grace make an interesting combination.

12

Praying Hands

The call to 911 came from an apartment complex where a downstairs resident had heard enraged fighting between a couple in the apartment above him. He had heard a "thump" – as though someone had hit the floor – then silence.

When we arrive, the officer knocks on the second floor apartment door. A young woman answers. The officer asks if she is OK, and she replies that she is. The officer asks if a man is in her apartment, and she says that he has left. Following standard procedure, the officer asks to come in to look around. In only a matter of minutes, he finds a young man hiding in the bedroom closet. During the ensuing 30 minutes, we listen to each person give their version of the story outside of earshot of the other.

Because the young woman has bruises on her face and cuts on her arms, the officer calls EMS to evaluate the seriousness of her wounds. The young man is arrested for assault, handcuffed, and placed in the backseat of the police cruiser for transport to the county jail.

Both young people are alarmingly casual about their contentious relationship. I sense that their lifestyle is a microcosm of our sinful world – filled with misguided priorities, lies, heated arguments, and violence.

As we often find when we respond to domestic calls, this apartment has few furnishings. Standing in an inconspicuous corner of the bland off-white sheet-rock walls is a bookcase. It has few books on its shelves, but on top is a prosaic color print of praying hands. The praying hands search for good in an evil world. They represent peace in contrast to conflict, goodness in contrast to confrontation, hope in contrast to anger, and mercy in contrast to emotional pain. They are an iconic reminder of God's presence.

Inside the apartment EMS prepares to transport the young victim to the hospital emergency room for treatment. When the gurney reaches the doorway, she glances up at the picture. She seems reflective, perhaps praying silently.

The abuser took no notice of the picture of the praying hands.

Outside, standing next to the police cruiser, I ask the officer, "Did you notice the praying hands on top of the book shelf?" He replies; "Yep, sure did." His cryptic acknowledgment of God's presence in a confrontational setting gives me hope in the midst of the pathological family violence before us.

13

Dreaded Dispatch

There is probably no greater pain for parents and family than the death of a child. Regardless of the age of the child, or the cause of death, the reality of a dead child is incomprehensible and unbearable.

On a Saturday morning about seven o'clock I am riding with the day shift. The officer and I are observing the normalcy of the day – quiet streets, little radio traffic, clear sky with no rain predicted. It's a nice start to a good day – a day that will soon turn ugly.

The radio crackles with a dispatcher requesting a Spanish-speaking officer for a "dead baby" call. It so happens that the officer I am with, Mario, is bilingual. Mario immediately radios 10-76 (en route). Mario activates his overhead lights into a "Code 2" mode (overhead strobe lights), accelerates his patrol unit and speeds from our assigned sector to the sector of the critical incident. I realize that this is the call I have always dreaded – the death of a child. My sinking feeling is common to all police, fire, and EMS personnel who are dispatched on such calls.

We arrive at the scene within ten minutes. A small crowd has gathered outside a small wooden frame house. The first officers on the scene are trying to communicate with the father and mother of the deceased infant. They are not making much progress in discerning details of what happened and when. Maria, the mother, is crying hysterically and speaks only Spanish. The father is still drunk from heavy drinking the night before.

Talking to the bilingual officer, Maria explains that she fed the baby about six that morning. She then took the child back to bed with her and her husband. A short time later she awakened to find the child listless and not breathing.

As Mario finishes his conversation with the mother, he turns to an Hispanic male neighbor who had been awakened by the mother's frantic screaming. The neighbor explains that, because he knew the family well, he immediately got out of bed and went next door to see what could be causing such hysterical screaming.

He found the door unlocked and discovered the baby lying on the bed seemingly without life. He grabbed the phone and called 911. Listening to the 911 operator, he began relaying instructions to Maria. She was told to place the baby on the floor and perform CPR until an EMS unit arrived. Maria, not trained in CPR techniques, followed the initial instructions to place the baby on the floor. In desperation the neighbor tried to convey the dispatcher's instructions. Unfortunately, Maria simply did not comprehend what her neighbor was telling her to do.

The father, in his drunken state, did little to help either the mother or the child.

While Mario translates information from the neighbor to Crime Scene Investigators (CSI), I approach Maria who is now on the front porch sitting between two female neighbors. Both are about the mother's age and have children of their own, judging by the tender way they are caring for the distraught mother.

One of the neighbor women is bilingual. Through her I try to comfort Maria, but to no avail. She is in complete denial that her baby is dead. She begs, pleads, and screams to hold her baby. I stand up, move off to the side and call my supervisor to request a bilingual Catholic priest. I have no indication that the family was Catholic, but I know that a Catholic Church is in the predominately Hispanic neighborhood and I am certain the priest is bilingual.

The priest arrives in a matter of minutes. As it turns out, I know him from previous community events. I brief him on the morning's events and identify Maria as the distressed mother. He is a skilled and experienced priest who quiets the mother for short periods of time only to be interrupted by new emotional eruptions.

The two police officers who were the first to arrive on scene are standing at the front door. I ask how they are doing. One officer says this is his "first dead baby call" and that he is struggling with his emotions. I can see why. Just inside the front door and lying on the floor in her white gown, the little baby girl looks like a doll that has been discarded by an older child. She will be left in place while CSI, detectives, and police photographers work the crime scene, The sight takes my breath away.

Like the Armed Services of this nation, most first responders – those on the front lines of war and critical incidents – are young. Most have wives or husbands. Many have young children. Time and again, I have heard first responders say that when they go home at shift's end following a critical incident involving children, they will seek out their child or children. They will hold them and love them for long periods of time.

Looking straight into the eyes of the inexperienced young officer, I say that all we can ask is that God comfort us through the love and compassion of family and community.

The inebriated father, who had been standing at curbside with his drinking buddies, breaks the somber moment when he approaches the front porch and asks the two officers if he can "come in to get a beer." Their reaction is swift and direct (with a few choice words) as they handcuff him and place him in the back seat of a patrol unit.

Stories Of The Street

The front yard and the street in front of the house are crowded with neighbors responding to the presence of multiple emergency vehicles. The rumor of a deceased baby has quickly spread among other young mothers in the community, and they hover around the baby's crying mother.

The investigation is completed and a detective is ready to carry the child from the crime scene to the waiting ambulance. The neighbors blessedly block the view of the sidewalk from the mother sitting at the end of the front porch. Victim Services personnel and the priest distract the mother by talking to her.

Suddenly the front screen door bursts open and a female detective hurriedly sprints out of the house, down the sidewalk, and enters the rear of the waiting ambulance. The human shield breaks down. The priest and Victim Services personnel become mute. Maria struggles to stand up while screaming for her baby. Everyone notices that the baby is wrapped in a pale pink baby blanket and lovingly held by the departing detective. The manner in which the detective holds the dead baby suggests she too is a mother.

The attending priest says in Spanish to the young and now childless mother – "You will see your baby again." His words fall on deaf ears.

> *A voice was heard in Ramah, wailing and loud lamentation, Rachel weeping for her children; she refused to be consoled, because they are no more.*[12]

The role of police chaplains is to care for and minister to police officers and police department staff. When we are inserted into a tragic event such as a "dead baby call," our job changes to a first responder role until Victim Services personnel arrive, or until the family pastor or priest is summoned and is on scene.

Subsequently I move my attention from Maria to the two officers who had arrived first and who were emotionally

---

[12] Jeremiah 31:15; Matthew 2:18 - NRSV

impacted by finding the dead baby. I can only imagine their feelings of helplessness in responding to the baby on the floor, and not being able to communicate with the parents. Did they try CPR on the baby or was it apparent the child was past resuscitation? How did they manage the hysterical Maria without being able to communicate with her due to the language barrier? What else could they have done before EMS and a bilingual officer arrived?

Their role changed dramatically from coping with a chaotic scene to guarding the front door of the house. EMS and CSI personnel must have protected boundaries in order to accomplish their responsibilities. How did the downgrade from first responder to guard duty impact the young officers' adrenaline? Did it influence their impatience toward the father when he inappropriately asked for access to his beer?

What really matters are the consequential emotions that may haunt officers and other first responders after a critical incident – especially the death of a child. For one of the two officers in this story, the early morning dispatch is his first "dead baby call." Of all the things that an officer or other first responders are exposed to, the death or abuse of a child is by far the worst. What was obvious is that both of these young officers were struggling with their emotions.

Did the emotional and mental health of these two young officers change? What emotional repercussions did they experience when they arrived home later that day? What did they say to their spouses and children about the incident; or did they keep it inside themselves, only adding to their emotional stress? How did they manage their probable sleeplessness that night and following nights as the image of the dead little girl lying on the floor in her white gown vividly replays itself over and over again in their minds?

I am confident that the two young officers involved with this call did not have the benefit of a formal Critical Incident Debriefing. (Reference Appendix) They likely had to rely on their own initiatives to find release from the stress associated with responding to such dreaded calls and seeing for the first time a lifeless baby lying on the floor – no wonder their worst fear is a "dead baby" call.

14

Where Was God Today?

We return to our sector after the infant death incident described in the previous story. Officer Mario has just finished writing his report on the deceased baby incident when dispatch radios:

"Nora 203."

Mario responds "Nora 203. Go ahead."

"House fire at 2301 Atlanta Street with possible person inside."

"10-4."

We are literally around the corner from the house fire. Within minutes Mario radios; "Nora 203, 10-23 (at scene) House filled with smoke, no flames showing."

"10-4."

Mario leaps from his patrol unit and races toward the front door. He kicks in the front door and enters the burning house only to return moments later empty-handed and choking on the dense smoke.

The sounds of sirens pierce the air as fire trucks come down the narrow neighborhood street. The ground shakes as the big trucks gear down to stop at the burning duplex. Firemen appear at the rear of the truck and begin pulling hoses toward the fireplug on the corner. Four firemen dressed in heavy gear with outer-space looking masks and oxygen tanks run to the house. Hysterical family and neighbors are screaming, "There is a crippled man inside!"

The four firefighters enter the small brown brick house through the same front door Mario had entered. So far there has not been a flame breakout from the house windows or its roof; only the dense gray smoke pouring from the doorway and broken windows.

In less than 30 seconds, the fire fighters burst from the front door carrying the victim. Each fireman is holding a limb of the paraplegic victim. Henry is naked, his skin dark gray and gritty from being in the heavy smoke. The four firemen lay him on the driveway. Firemen immediately begin administering oxygen and CPR. Henry remains uncovered as the fire fighters apply their life-saving skills, trying desperately to find signs of life.

EMS personnel arrive and take over the revival efforts. They continue CPR on Henry for at least 20 minutes. Acknowledging Henry's lifeless body and the absence of any visible response, EMS technicians mercifully place him on a gurney and move him to a waiting ambulance. Although an EMS technician continues chest compressions during the transfer from the driveway to the waiting ambulance, it is for the benefit of the family and neighbors only. Henry is DOS (dead on scene).

The tragedy began when Henry's wife, his daughter and her two sons, ages seven and three, arrive home from the grocery store. They are horrified to see their house on fire. They begin screaming and become frantic to rescue Henry. They know he cannot physically escape the burning duplex. The boys are terrified.

Henry's daughter is torn between the efforts to rescue her dad and tending to her children. I identify myself as a police chaplain and ask if she wants me to care for the three-year old. She hands me the little boy and I walk away from the drama. The engines of the large fire trucks, along with their massive pumps create a heavy and unrelenting roar. The terrified child cries in panic for "his mommy." Within a few minutes a neighbor takes the child and leaves the scene.

My attention now turns to the victim's wife who had been seated in a lawn chair only feet away from the CPR rescue attempt. She is wailing and confused by all the chaos around her. Her daughter, son-in-law, and Victim Services personnel are doing their best to comfort her.

An EMS female attending Henry's wife stands up and asks me to assist them in telling her that her husband is dead. When I bend down at her side, she sees the Chaplain insignia on my shirt and the crosses on my collar. She has a violent and uncontrollable reaction – screaming, kicking, and combative. The EMS supervisor on scene nods to his staff and they immediately secure her on the gurney with its wide restraining straps, give her a sedative injection, and load her into a second ambulance on scene. She is transported to the emergency room at the trauma hospital where she will be evaluated and kept overnight.

The ambulance leaves. The scene is strangely quiet with all the pumps and diesel engines either gone or turned off. In surveying the scene I notice Henry's seven-year-old grandson leaning against a police unit some 20 yards down the street. He has distanced himself from the frantic effort to save his grandfather and from the violent reaction of his grandmother. He is turning inward. I remember that some psychologists say that between ages six and ten years, a child begins to understand the meaning of death and its biological aspects.

I join him. We lean against the PD patrol unit. He does not want to talk about his grandfather other than to say how much he loved him. He is worried that his grandfather is hurt. I agree with him. "Your granddad is hurt really bad but the doctors and nurses at the hospital are doing everything they can to help him." He nods. I do not feel he can handle learning that his grandfather is dead, especially without his parents close by to console him.

The boy and I walk away from the police car and move toward the fenced backyard where two puppies are eager for the boy's attention. Their tails wag vigorously while they jump up and down along the fence line.

The boy bends over, and as he pets the loving animals, he recounts when he and his mother, grandmother, and little brother came home from the grocery store. He talks about what he saw when they came down the street to see their house on fire.

Since what Henry's grandson is telling me is important, I take the boy to the fire inspector whose responsibility is to determine the origin of the fire. He asks the boy: Were the doors of the house locked or unlocked? Was anything left cooking on the kitchen stove? Did his granddaddy smoke?

Henry's grandson finishes telling his story to the fire inspector. His dad and mom join him and embrace him. His dad picks him up and he and his parents leave the devastation and chaos of the death scene.

But questions still remain. Why did Henry crawl to the back door when his bed was less than eight feet away from the front door? Is this an accident scene or a crime scene?

After the family, neighbors, and on-lookers drift away from the scene, the fire inspector instructs firemen to bring the victim's bed outside in the daylight for closer examination. Then the bed reveals its secrets. The mattress is burned except where the paraplegic had laid. The area was in sharp contrast to the rest of the burnt mattress. Lying on the margin of the unburned area was a charred book of matches and a crack pipe. The inspector concludes the fire originated in bed resulting in a horrible death for the deceased. Paralyzed and perhaps influenced by crack cocaine, Henry became confused in his panic to escape. In the dense smoke he pulled himself along the floor in the wrong direction. The fireman found his body at the back door on the opposite side of the house from his bed.

Mario and I are quiet as we resume the day shift in our sector. Mario had been dispatched to only two calls during the entire shift on this day. The first was the "dead baby" call; the second, the fire death of the paraplegic. I break the silence with a question addressed to myself as much as to Mario: "Where was God today?"

We both are silent as we individually ponder the question. Then he responds, "I don't know."

I am not sure I know either. Perhaps God was in the sad eyes of the seven-year-old boy as he leaned against the police unit, watching the horrific scene surrounding his grandfather. Perhaps God was in the new life of Henry's puppies that gave the young boy hope.

Perhaps God was visible in the female detective who tenderly and lovingly carried the dead baby wrapped in a pale pink blanket to the waiting ambulance.

Perhaps God's mercy was given through first responders at the two scenes; i.e., the compassion of police officers and EMS personnel. Perhaps mercy went in with firemen who entered a burning building to retrieve Henry. Perhaps mercy went in with the chaplain and Victim Services personnel who tried to bring comfort in the midst of pain and emptiness.

Mercy was there and God was there.

Mario: "Nora 203."

Dispatch: "Go ahead."

Mario: "10-42." (End of duty)

Dispatch: "10-4."

Street Images III

God's Face Stories

"God makes his face to shine upon you and be gracious to you"

Numbers 6

15

The Rookie Cop
(Three Parts)

Most individuals who seek a career in law enforcement do so because of the "sense of call." The thrill of an engaging career, the lure of driving high-tech police cruisers, the recognition for heroic arrests or life-saving actions – all have their role in inspiring the personal call to public service. More importantly, commissioned police officers have a sense of call to serve a community.

There is an analogy between being called to a role in public service as a police officer and that of being called to the ministry. The sense of call for both professions is to serve others and to influence the well-being of society and the communities they serve.

In their book <u>The Power of the Call,</u> Henry Brandt and Henry T. Blackaby write about God's eternal purposes entrusted to persons to manage His "treasure" and to respond obediently as He instructs and guides them on His mission to redeem a lost world. They pointedly explain the seriousness of the power of one's call when they write:

> You are the custodian of the most important information in the world...your divine calling far supercedes all other professions...the call and the enabling are special. Do not let anyone explain away our high calling, and make it common to all. It is not common! [13]

Jena is an attractive young woman with a beautiful complexion and coal-black hair pulled tightly against her head and folded in a bun at the back. She is a person of warmth and charm. She is well liked and respected by her peers and the community she serves. In high school she was a police department intern. When Jena graduated, she applied to the police academy to continue her sense of call and become a public servant. While still a teenager, Jena already knew exactly what she wanted to do with her life.

A police academy is a six to nine-month training program with an intense course of study and physical preparation. Jena and her cadet friends were confronted with detailed criminal and civil law codes, police policy and procedures, city ordinances, family and domestic violence psychology, plus the ever-present weekly tests measuring each student's absorption and progression of the academy's curriculum.

Physical fitness demands, arrest and handcuffing techniques, hand-to-hand street fighting, and weapon training compound the stressors of becoming a well-trained and capable police officer.

> Without realizing it, the rookie officer is taking on a new identity as much as he or she is beginning a new career. By now, hardly anyone considers this just a job. Excitement is high; anxiety is up. Bonding with fellow rookies for practical help and social support eases the anxiety about completing the course. Depending on coworkers will become a lifelong habit,

---

[13] The Power of the Call, Henry T. Blackaby and Henry Brandt, Broadman & Holman Publishers, Nashville, Tennessee, 1997, pp. 22, 28

one that is considered to be critical to survival in the job and on the street.[14]

Jena was a rookie cop when I first met her. She was well-trained, professional, and committed in her call to public service. I remember her rolling down her patrol unit's windows and speaking to the children waiting at school-bus corners. They would wave and react with youthful glee at seeing "Officer Jena" each morning.

Jena is on patrol. The sun is bright, the air cool. The time is mid afternoon on a beautiful November day. Jena has no idea that the impending dispatch to a fatality wreck would set off a chain of events that would change her life forever. Although the events were unrelated to each other, they had a common denominator – violent death.

Part One – My First – The Loss of Innocence

Jena glances at her inboard and outboard rear-view mirrors for traffic approaching from behind her. She changes her focus to oncoming traffic, and seeing that all is clear, performs a tight U-turn. The tires of the patrol unit squeal under the centrifugal force of the sudden turn. Activating her overheads (emergency light bar mounted on top of patrol units) and her siren, Jena speeds toward the "wreck with injuries" dispatch she has received. She is tense at the probability that she will be the first on scene at a violent death. Her stomach churns as she realizes this is her first fatality dispatch as a police officer.

The probability turns to reality. She is in fact the first police officer to arrive. In front of her is an 18-wheeler gravel truck with long streaks of burnt rubber marking a trail of locked air brakes. The truck is loaded with crushed limestone

---

[14] I Love a Cop – What Police Families Need to Know, Ellen Kirschman, Ph.D., The Guilford Press, New York and London, 2006, p. 33

on its way to a construction site. Jena's first thought is: "How bad?"

In the roadway ditch is a light-colored four-door sedan with its driver's side caved in. The impact of the 18-wheeler had driven the sedan into an embankment, creating a bowl-shaped depression matching the shape and size of the sedan. Inside is Kathryn, an elderly woman dressed in fall colors. A pumpkin-colored blouse and dark brown skirt are spattered in blood and shattered glass. Kathryn is gasping desperately for each breath. She has a blank stare on her face as Jena maneuvers her way inside the passenger side of the car to gain assess to the dying victim.

Technically, Kathryn is not a "pin-in" requiring a "Jaws-of-Life" rescue attempt. Nevertheless she is entangled in crushed metal, fiberglass panels, and glass from the shattered windshield and driver-side window. The spider-web fracture of safety glass casts distorted hues of sunlight on Kathryn's pale face.

Jena gains limited access to the critically injured woman. Waiting on EMS units seems to take a lifetime. She holds the elderly woman tenderly stroking her forehead with loving hands. Kathryn looks into Jena's eyes, takes her last breath, and dies in Jena's arms.

The rookie Jena lamented later, "I watched her die. I saw her take her last breath. Why couldn't I fix this?" Jena's words trailed off as the memory of this deadly accident rushed back.

Police department policy states that the first officer on a scene is the primary reporting officer. The officer must recount the events in writing and file a formal Police Report with the police chain of command and legal officials. Because Jena is the first officer on the scene she is charged with writing the critical incident report. Jena interviews the truck driver, Jesse, and other witnesses, and takes photographs documenting her written words. She learns from Jesse that Kathryn had appropriately stopped at the cross-over intersection, then pulled out in front of him, apparently not seeing his huge rig bearing down on her. The distraught Jesse says, "She looked directly at me in horror as she realized I was going to hit her broadside."

Jena told me later, "When I returned to my patrol car and prepared to write my report, I thought about how tragic the lady's death was. It was the Tuesday before Thanksgiving and I could only imagine the devastation her family would feel over her death."

This was the rookie cop's first violent death where she is the first responder on the scene. Because she was the first officer on scene, she was responsible for properly preparing the required documentation including photographs of the scene. The combination of these factors contributed to Jena's becoming emotional at police headquarters at the end-of-shift debriefing. "I kept asking myself, 'Why do these things happen?' Watching this sweet lady die in my arms kept replaying itself in my mind."

The day after Thanksgiving, Jena's chief asked that I ride out with Jena. He was concerned about Jena's coping with her first violent death experience. The next day I rode with Jena and she admitted her distress over Kathryn's death. She told me, "I did not sleep at all the night of the incident. I kept seeing the elderly lady's face as she died. This was my first death scene. I will never forget it."

Jena drove us to the scene. We got out of her patrol car and she pointed out to me the bowl-shaped depression in the embankment where Kathryn's car came to rest. Her eyes were focused on the embankment as she relived the moments she spent inside the car with the dying Kathryn. Jena was pensive, silent.

Quietly I asked Jena; "Would you like a prayer?" She replied "Yes". Instinctively I place my arm around her waist. I pray:

> Merciful God, we lift up your servant Kathryn in her tragic death. We pray that she has found peace in your kingdom free from all trauma, fear, and pain. We pray for Jesse as he surely struggles with the memory

of locked brakes, the horror on Kathryn's face, and the moment of impact. We pray a prayer of thanksgiving for Jena's compassion in giving Kathryn comfort with God's love as she slipped into eternity. We pray, O God, that Jena will be strengthened by her faith, and by her courage in the face of this traumatic event. We pray our prayer in your Precious and Holy Name. Amen.

The shift we spent together appropriately served as a critical incident debriefing (discussed in more detail in the Appendix) that allowed Jena to talk about her role in the fatal wreck, including her emotional reactions. She knew she was in a trustworthy setting. She knew that I would respect these holy moments.

Part Two – Not Again – The Loss of Naiveté

Five days after Kathryn died, on the Sunday following Thanksgiving Day, my phone rings at 5:45 a.m. I am already dressed in clerical shirt and collar and prepared for the 9 a.m. worship service at the parish where I serve as pastor. The call is from the police department dispatcher reporting a suicide had just occurred. The dispatcher asks that I report to the death scene as soon as possible. With the address and directions in hand, I tell my wife where I am going and leave the house.

The reflective letters "P O L I C E" on the side of a vehicle in the driveway caught my eye as I drove the darkened street. Arriving at the home, I am surprised to see my friend and rookie cop Jena talking to Irma, a woman in her seventies who is in total distress. Jena looks at me with eyes that are saying "Not again – so soon." Jena nods toward the hallway that leads to the bedroom. She is clearly sending the message: "The body is that way." Because of my clerical shirt, Irma immediately comes toward me. We sit down at the dining room table and she numbly begins to share her story. She cries softly into a white tissue she is holding.

My husband killed himself. He is in the guestroom closet.

I ignored all the signs. He gave away his pickup truck; he gave me a detailed description of the funeral he wanted; he kept saying the end was near. I thought he was referring to his constant and severe pain from his pancreatic cancer. The doctor had just told us he was rapidly deteriorating. I am so sorry I failed him. I am so sorry.

Vernon woke me earlier this morning and said he wanted me to go out to the patio with him. I got up and we sat down in our chairs and looked out into the darkness. He asked if we could say the Lord's Prayer. We did. We went back into the house and back to bed. I went back to sleep immediately.

I was awakened by a gunshot. I didn't know where it came from and I was not sure it was a gunshot – but it sounded like one. I couldn't find Vernon. I looked outside on the patio; he was not there. I looked again in our bedroom and saw what looked like a person in Vernon's hospital bed. It was not – only pillows stacked to look like a person in bed. I panicked. I ran through the house yelling his name. No answer. I began to look in the closets. I opened the closet door in the guestroom and I saw him; headless, blood everywhere. I was sick to my stomach. I called 911.

Only now does Irma begin to put together all the pieces of the past few days. A sense of guilt and shame seems to sweep over her for not recognizing the indications that Vernon was suicidal. She tells me that Vernon no longer wanted to fight against the painful end-stage cancer. Irma continues to cry softly as she methodically begins to dial the phone numbers of family and close friends.

Giving her space to speak with family members, I walk over to Jena. She tells me how uncomfortable she was waiting for other first responders to arrive. "I did not know what to say to her. She asked me if her husband was going to heaven. I didn't know how to answer her. My own mother always told me and my brothers and sisters that suicide was an unforgivable sin and a person killing himself or herself was destined to hell. I am thinking 'what a way to end life.' I felt a great sorrow for her."

Jena's police training had taught her to put on her "game face" in critical incidents. Police work is an emotional labor and an officer breaking down only exacerbates a critical incident and destroys first responder leadership.

> From the beginning, cops are taught to maintain an occupational persona: a 'public face' that makes them always appear to be in control, on top of things, knowledgeable, and unafraid. In fact, much of the stress of police work is a result of trying to hide the stress of the job. [15]

Following police policy, Jena is again the designated officer who is to write the police report of another critical incident involving a violent death scene. Because of Jena's first violent death experience fresh in the minds of her peers, experienced officers attempt to shield her from the ghoulish scene and from the demands placed on her as the officer in charge of the scene.

Jena recalled later that she told the two backup officers in frustration, "I do not like being shielded from my job. Let me do it! You will not be here all the time and I have to do it," referring to the work of writing reports, taking crime scene pictures, talking to witnesses. "And so the two officers stepped aside and I made my notes, took the necessary pictures, and watched as funeral home personnel picked up the headless

---

[15] I Love a Cop – What Police Families Need to Know, Ellen Kirschman, Ph.D., The Guilford Press, New York, London, 2006, pg.18

body, pieces of skull, brain matter, and shattered teeth. The smell of gun residue permeated the closet. It's funny, but I distinctly remember them taking off his watch from his headless body."

Irma and Vernon's home is now full of family, neighbors, first responders, and funeral home personnel. An uncomfortable awkwardness fills the air as people do not know what to say to Irma, or to each other. I seek out Irma and privately tell her how sorry I am for her loss and give her assurance of God's presence in her time of need. In a soft voice, I pray with her for courage and grace to fill her days as the realization of Vernon's tragic death becomes omnipresent.

It is now 8:30 a.m. I excuse myself and leave for the worship service that begins in 30 minutes.

There are no secrets in the first responder community due to radio traffic among local police, EMS, and fire entities. A first responder who is a member of the church asks a question: "Were you there?"

We both know what he was referring to.

I reply; "Yes."

"Was it bad?"

"Yes, really bad."

The bell rings in the church steeple above us, the organist begins the first hymn, and I begin my walk behind the acolytes to the front of the church. Polished silver vessels containing the elements of Holy Communion sit with dignity on the white altar linens.

The polished brass cross on the altar seems more brilliant than usual. It is like a beacon drawing me to its glory while at the same time giving off a gentle peace and a respite from evil. Behind the altar is a standing life-size figure of Jesus with arms outstretched, beckoning me with the gospel words: *"Come to me, all of you that are weary and are carrying heavy burdens, and I will give you rest."*[16] I am in awe in this setting. It is a

---

[16] Matthew 11:28 - NSRV

profound contrast to the scene I witnessed less than an hour earlier.

In an interview with Jena some years later she rationalized, "Although I showed no emotion at the suicide scene it definitely bothered me. I still carry it with me. I cannot forget it. I used to be fascinated with crime scene photography. Not now! I no longer seek out the gore."

The days before and following Thanksgiving will be forever etched in Jena's mind. However, her embedded images of that holiday violence will soon pale in contrast to what happens to the rookie cop during the season of Christmas two weeks later.

Part Three – I Plead with Him to Tell Me the Truth

The Loss of a Family Member

It is mid-morning on December 15 and the department store is busy with Christmas shoppers. Officer Jena is working on her day off at the store to earn extra money to help pay her mom's bills and to provide a few extra gifts for her young family.

Unexpectedly, Jena's brother shows up at the store and announces abruptly to Jena, "Mom is missing."

Jena asks, equally abruptly, "What do you mean, missing?"

He replies, "She's not at home. I can't find her anywhere."

Without hesitating, Jena excuses herself with the store manager and leaves for the home of her mother.

The house is unusually clean except for her mother's room that appears in total disarray. Jena notices the smell of bleach but doesn't think anything of it. She recalls her mind being hammered with alternating thoughts about the horrific suicide she had worked just a few weeks earlier and her mother recently threatening to kill herself because she couldn't pay her bills.

At the time of her mother's threat, Jena called the police department for assistance. Jena's peers showed up at her mother's house, causing an immediate angry response from her mother. In the confrontation that followed, her mother, in a rage, pushed Jena out the front door of the house. As Jena fell backwards, a fellow officer caught her while jamming his foot in the doorway preventing her mother from slamming it shut. The officer talked to Jena's mother for over 30 minutes. Later, in the privacy of his patrol car, he told Jena that her mother was not likely to kill herself.

This incident keeps playing in Jena's mind as she and other family members begin to widen the search for her missing mother. "That was the last time I saw my mom."

Police and fire department personnel, family, friends, plus over 200 citizen volunteers diligently search the entire community and then into the surrounding countryside. Even a national volunteer search firm joined the search bringing its expertise in finding missing persons. Nothing is found — no clothing, purse, shoes — nothing.

Jena lamented that her Mom had just disappeared. Yet, there were not any clues or tips associated with the disappearance. Jena could not comprehend that her Mom would just vanish without a trace: "There is no way Mom would walk away from family and her grandchildren during Christmas."

Police officers are extremely sensitive to personal nuances and behavior patterns of people. Jena is no exception. She noticed that her brother was "acting weird." Other family members agreed. With heartache, Jena made the decision to go to her police supervisor with her family's suspicions.

Three weeks after her disappearance the body of Officer Jena's mother is discovered in an abandoned barn.

It was the responsibility of the Police Chief to deliver the death notification to his rookie officer. The Chief would later comment; "What police administrator ever thinks that they will have to deliver the message to one of their employees that the employee's mother was the victim of a homicide? In my wildest and worst dreams I could never have imagined that would be my plight. The presence and support of a police chaplain assisted me through this very difficult job and time."

The discovery of her mother's body immediately caused a dramatic physical reaction for Jena. The stressors of two previous violent deaths, aggravated by her mother's murder, caused serious gastrointestinal distress. She found herself caught in an untenable tension between her role as a police officer and her loyalty to her brother who was now considered a suspect in the murder of their mother.

The suspected brother remained firm in his denial of any involvement in the disappearance and murder of their mother. Under serious and intense interrogation, including surveillance-camera pictures of him buying rope at a hardware store that matched the rope found with the body, he still maintained his innocence. As Jena observed later, "His story contained unexplained gaps that were not consistent with previous comments he made."

Investigating officers asked Jena to interview her brother. They were hopeful he would confess to Jena. And if he did confess, Jena's police training and professional expertise would enable her to follow the procedures that would ensure a grand jury indictment for murder against him.

In an interrogation room, Jena confronted her brother with the facts about their mother's murder. He avoided looking at her. With his head down, arms resting on his knees, he stared silently at the floor.

Jena pleaded with him, "Tell me the truth!" He said nothing.

Although the family was now convinced more than ever of their brother's guilt, the police did not arrest him because the district attorney was seeking a confession before taking the case to a Grand Jury.

Jena appealed to the police. "You think, we think, he did it. Do something! Arrest him!"

Jena was stressed between an all-but-certain involvement by her own brother and her understanding of the district attorney's insistence on a confession. Despite her gut feeling of her brother's role in the murder, she told him that he could stay with her in her home while the investigation continued.

She explained, "I will stand by him till proven guilty." Then she paused. "I am on guard as he moves his stuff to my house. I lock my bedroom door at night and keep my weapon on the bed with me. I am still trying to convince myself that my brother did not kill our mother."

Confronted with overwhelming evidence against him and the increasing emotion of guilt, Albert notified police that he would be at Jena's house to meet with his family. Because of her professional relationship with the police department, police officials agreed to give the family space while at the same time forming a perimeter around the house and yard to prevent an escape. Their presence also would provide protection for the family should the event turn ugly.

Albert confessed to his family in an emotional scene in the backyard. He spilled out his guilt to his grieving family.

Albert: "Mom and I were arguing. She slapped me. I lost it. I did it. I strangled her."

Officer Jena: "Was it quick for her? Did she suffer?"

Albert: "No. She didn't suffer."

Jena: "You have taken so much from us. You dropped mom's body like an animal."

The scene quickly accelerated into a family disturbance causing the waiting police officers to intervene. Albert was arrested, handcuffed, placed in a police car, and transported to jail. He wrote the formal confession sought by the district attorney.

Rev. Steve Best

Jena:

He broke my heart. When I saw him on TV in handcuffs, my vomiting started again. I felt fear for him in prison. I hurt for him. I fear him. We were raised that if we could not be friends with our own brothers and sisters, you could not be friends with others. I cannot hate him. Anger, yes. I still think there are things he is hiding – things that would bring closure for me although it would bring more pain to my brother and my sister.

I have my days. I see my Mom in what I do for my kids. Yet, we are without the little things that grandmothers do for children. My children will never know their grandmother.

My sister and I have forgiven Albert for what he did to our family. Although we will always grieve for our loss, we remain in contact with him through letters and occasional phone calls. Other family members may never be able to forgive. I wish they could because only then will they find peace.

In his book, What's So Amazing About Grace?[17] Philip Yancey says; "magnanimous forgiveness [as expressed by Jena and her sister] allows the possibility of transformation."

To emphasize his point, Yancy quotes Louis Smedes:

You think of him [a perpetrator] now not as the person who hurt you, but a person who needs you. You feel him now not as the person who alienated you, but as the person who belongs to you. Once you branded him as a person powerful in evil, but now you see him as a person weak in his needs. You recreated

---

[17] What's So Amazing About Grace; Zondervan Publishing House, Grand Rapids, MI, 1997, p. 102

your past by recreating the person whose wrong made your past painful.[18]

Throughout a period of extraordinary stress Police Officer Jena continued to work her shift with the courage and discipline expected of an officer of the law.

Did she see herself and her family as victims? Yes.

Did she experience human emotions and physical stressors? Yes.

Did she present herself as being immune to human frailties? No.

Did Jena go 10-42 – "out of service"? No.

Amid the time of her perseverance at work, rookie police officer Jena experienced her first fatality wreck scene; followed by a disturbing and bloody suicide scene; followed by the vicious murder of her own mother and the trial of her brother. During all this time, Jena honored the delicate balance between her duty as a commissioned police officer and her own personal reactions to violent death.

In her book <u>I Love a Cop</u>, Ellen Kirschman writes:

> Cops and their families hate to think of themselves as victims: A victim is someone else. Cops solve problems; they don't have them. This is one of the paradoxes of the police subculture: At times police demand to be seen as fully human, and at other times they reject that notion and hold themselves to be immune to human frailty. Immunity is one of the illusions that is lost or temporarily "out of service" following a trauma.[19]

The Police Department Victims Service Unit took over the responsibility of providing counseling and care for Jena's

---

[18] <u>Forgiveness: the Power to Change the Past</u>; Lewis B. Smedes, Christianity Today, January 7, 1983, p. 24

[19] <u>I Love a Cop – What Police Families Need to Know</u>, Ellen Kirschman, Ph.D., The Guilford Press, New York, London, 2006, p. 78

family for months throughout the discovery, funeral, arrest, and trial. The department also did all the paperwork with the Attorney General's Office for the Victim Compensation Act that paid for the funeral. Jena was grateful. "The Department was a big help to us."

Patrol Officer Jena is no longer a rookie cop. She is a seasoned police officer that is empathetic toward families suffering from a myriad of causes for human sadness. She is acutely aware of the image of the human condition.

She is also a disciplined police officer who enforces the laws of her city, state, and country. And, she still rolls down the window of her patrol car in school zones for the children to wave at Officer Jena – and she waves back with her endearing smile.

16

Alcohol, Distraction, and Death

It is a dark night. The time is a few minutes after midnight. The lighting on the entrance ramps to the freeway loop is minimal. A twenty-something young woman named Leslie has been to a party at a girlfriend's home. They had a good time drinking, laughing, and telling their own stories of love, break-ups, and all the repercussions of hopefulness mixed with disappointments of youthful romance.

Leslie approaches the westbound entrance ramp of the loop. As she drives, she picks up her cell phone and calls her boyfriend at work. Bud is a fire fighter assigned to a station located on the west side of town. He is on duty and has himself been telling stories to his fellow fire fighters. His stories, though, are about the troubled relationship he has with Leslie.

Bud answers his cell phone. Leslie explains she is on the way home and wants to stop by the fire station to use the restroom. Bud, irritated by Leslie's request, grudgingly agrees to meet her at the door of the fire station. He turns to his buddies and vigorously complains about her stopping by the station.

Leslie has returned her cell phone to her purse and turns right onto the ramp. Unfortunately, she has driven past the entrance to the westbound ramp during the phone call. Without realizing her mistake, she is now traveling west on the eastbound side of the loop.

She approaches a moderate hill on the loop and at the top meets an oncoming car in the inside lane. She swerves, as does the other driver, and the two cars scrape sides as they pass each other.

What happens next is predictable. She now is in the outside lane where a large three-quarter-ton pickup truck is approaching. The two vehicles collide head-on. Leslie is killed instantly.

Police dispatch receives a 911 call from a citizen that a bad wreck has occurred in the eastbound lanes of the loop on the south side of town.

Police, EMS, and the fire department deploy immediately. The fire department lieutenant on duty, aware of Bud's telephone conversation with Leslie, is concerned the call might involve Leslie. He tells the fire fighters in his vehicle that if his concerns prove true, they are to keep Bud from the wrecked vehicles.

When the fire responders reach the accident scene, the red paint of Leslie's vehicle is visible, but the car itself is a shapeless mass in the twisted metal with the pickup. The lieutenant immediately assigns Bud to support duty that keeps him away from the carnage. Shortly, the lieutenant will drive Bud to police headquarters to await the victim's identity.

Police headquarters at 12:30 a.m. is a quiet and lonely place. Other than officers who stop by occasionally during their shift, the only person in the building is the 911 operator/dispatcher. She hears the radio traffic that Bud is being brought to the station. She knows he will be alone in the training room when the identity of the deceased female is confirmed. She knows the odds are high that the victim is Bud's girlfriend. She pages me as the police chaplain on call.

My pager awakens me with its high decibel beeps at 12:35 a.m. I call police dispatch and listen to a female voice explain,

Stories Of The Street

"There has been a fatality on the loop and we need you at the police station as soon as possible."

Years ago an experienced pastor told me that he used to become panicky when he received emergency calls to come to a death scene or a hospital. But experience taught him to take his time and consider what his role and responsibility would be when he arrived at the scene or the hospital. He said that by taking time to listen "to God be God," he would invariably arrive with calmness, and with an ability to discern how best to serve the victims and/or their families.

I remember this advice each time I am summoned to critical incidents. This case would be no different. In a solemn mood I slowly put on my police chaplain shirt, my trousers and shoes. I know full well that my wife is awake and recognizes that something serious has happened. I hug her, tell her there has been a fatality wreck on the loop, kiss her goodnight, and open the door to the garage. As I drive to police headquarters, I pray for guidance and the wisdom to address the needs of whomever I am being called to help. My seminary professor's words ring in my ears again and again: "Remember, YOU are the God person in the room."

The front door of police headquarters is unlocked in expectation of impending arrivals. I enter the building, walk to the interior security door, key in the security code, and walk to the dispatch control room. The dispatcher briefs me on what has happened as she understands it from the radio traffic.

She also tells me that a fire department lieutenant has arrived with a fireman minutes earlier and that they are in the training room. Our eyes meet for just a second as we both realize the gut-wrenching event that is occurring on the loop and in the training room. I nod, she smiles, and I turn to leave the dispatch center for the training room.

Looking through the long rectangular glass window in the training room door, I see a lieutenant sitting in a chair directly in front of a fireman. His head is down and the lieutenant's facial expression is serious as he leans forward to talk to the young man. I wait until the lieutenant relaxes his posture before knocking softly, then opening the door.

The lieutenant looks relieved when he sees me. Bud looks up; his expression does not change. The lieutenant stands up, pats Bud on the shoulder, and tells him that he will help him any way he can. Glancing at me, he nods and leaves the room.

Police ministry is a *ministry of presence.* Bud's body language is clearly saying he does not want to talk or be talked to. For that reason I place a chair off his right shoulder and slightly behind him – close enough for him to know I am there, far enough away so as to not intrude into his private space. In a soft voice I say; "I'm sorry, Bud." His head moves slightly acknowledging my presence.

Silence.

One of the most difficult gifts for a pastor to cultivate is the patience to remain silent in a totally silent environment. Often we feel compelled to talk about life, death, and eternal life, invariably leading to quoting Scripture.

In response to the intrusion into their private space, a grieving person who wants to be left alone usually tunes the pastor out with a polite smile or with a look of aggravation that communicates, "Leave me alone!" Settings such as the one I find myself in with Bud will always separate police chaplains who are "good listeners" from those who are aggressive "soul savers."

The wall clock seems to crawl its way around its dial. Bud remains motionless in the plastic classroom chair, his elbows on his knees, his forehead resting in his hands. Forty long minutes into his grief processing, he begins to talk in an almost inaudible and resigned voice. He tells of the struggles he and Leslie were working their way through the past few weeks. He talks about her cell phone call at midnight and his irritation that she wanted to stop at the station to relieve herself. He confesses that his irritation got the best of him, and that after he hung up, he belittled Leslie to his fellow firefighters.

Now he grieves the loss of his companion and regrets the way he talked to her and about her in what turned out to be his last contact with her. He sobs softly, tears escaping from beneath his hands in which he has buried his face.

"Would you like a prayer?" I ask. He nods his approval.

In a whispered tone:

> God of Mercy, we don't understand why life has been taken from Leslie. We pray that your mercy be bestowed upon her. Receive Leslie into your kingdom, endear her with your love, and bless her with eternal peace.
>
> We lift up your servant Bud, that you will give him physical and spiritual courage in the days and weeks ahead. Relieve him of any burden of guilt, and give him the peace of your understanding and grace.
>
> We pray for his friends who now care for Leslie and will soon provide care for Bud through their friendship and compassion. Bless them and sustain them and Bud in their service to this community.
>
> We pray in the Name of Jesus, Amen.

Silence returns to the room.

Sometime after 2:00 a.m. the door to the training room opens and a young man breathes, "Bud?" Bud lifts his head, turns and sees his brother in the doorway. The two brothers meet in a warm embrace. Bud's frame trembles as his grief pours out on his brother's shoulder. The brother says, "Let's go, Bud. I'll take you home."

Bud has yet to make eye contact with me. But now he turns, revealing his tear-stained face. He extends his hand and says, "Thank you, Chaplain, for being here." The two men walk out of the room together, their heads tilted downward, the loving brother's arm draped over Bud's shoulders.

Over the past decade national, state, and municipal first responder agencies have built a model to help first responders cope with the tragedies they see first-hand in their duties. The model is called Critical Incident Stress Management (CISM). (Reference Appendix)

Police departments have taken the lead in developing the CISM programs with fire and EMS units following suit. The International Conference of Police Chaplains and state departments of public safety now provide certification for both basic and advanced training in CISM. In preparation for my service, I received basic and advanced training with the Texas Department of Public Safety and served as a member of the DPS Critical Incident Response Teams (CIRT).

There are two major components in addressing CISM. (Reference Appendix). The first is called a *debriefing* in which all first responders and CISM peer team members review the incident in detail, with each responder having the opportunity to describe his/her role at the scene and how they reacted to the stress they endured. Debriefings are generally held 24 to 72 hours following the incident.

The second component of CISM fills an immediate need for first responders to talk though their roles and responses immediately following the event. This form of stress management is called a *defusing*. (Reference Appendix). This was the case for the fatality involving young Leslie.

Both approaches include first responders telling their version of the event and their emotional feelings of stress, including guilt, anger, not doing enough to save a life, etc. There is a time for the leader to discuss symptoms of stress that may appear later such as loss of sleep, impatience, withdrawal, dependence on alcohol or drugs, and other physical and emotional reactions. Suggestions to normalize deep-seated feelings are then offered to the responders with the encouragement to commit to a healthy physical and mental regimen for one's own good health in a tough and demanding job.

The fire department's first responders were brought to the police department's training room, the same room Bud and I shared for several hours. Their purpose was to participate in a CISM defusing. Each fireman told about his role at the scene and how he was dealing with the stress and anxiety of the accident. The anxieties ran high because of Leslie's death, a person they personally knew and who was an important person in the life of Bud, their friend and shift mate. This portion of the defusing lasted over an hour as the nine firemen talked through their personal stories and emotions.

The defusing moved toward closure with the posture and demeanor of the young men seemingly relaxed and subdued in contrast to their anxiety and uncertainty at the beginning of the session. I suggested we close with the Lord's Prayer and the firemen, without any direction from me, stood up and began to reach for the hand of the adjacent fireman. I was truly moved as the young men, in their fire-department uniforms and holding hands, prayed the Lord's Prayer in unison.

The young men began to leave to return to their station. Their lieutenant, the man who alertly spared Bud from additional trauma by removing him from the wreck scene, stops at the doorway and says to me, "In all my years in firefighting I have never been a part of such a substantive session. It is obvious to me that my people needed to be here and to have an opportunity to express their feelings. Thank you, Chaplain, for helping us begin the process of healing."

It is well after 3:00 a.m. in the morning. I begin my trip home at a deliberate and slow pace, contemplating the events of the past three hours. I cannot help but offer a prayer of thanksgiving for God's presence in the training room tonight – the wisdom given me to not invade Bud's space, the wisdom to listen to his story without prejudice or judgment, and the strength to lead the defusing in a pastoral manner. I pray that my presence during the events of this critical incident will contribute to the well-being of the young first responders.

As I enter our home, I pause again to thank God that my loving wife is unharmed and safely asleep in our bed.

Rev. Steve Best

17

Katrina: The Power of Commitment (Five Parts)

The Texas Department of Public Safety (Texas DPS) deploys Critical Incident Response Teams (CIRT) to scenes involving major disasters, violent deaths, horrific crime scenes, and other critical incidents that impact the lives of first responders. In cases of national disasters, the Texas DPS CIRT may be deployed upon request if DPS resources and personnel are available.

Such was the case in the aftermath of Hurricane Katrina, which devastated New Orleans and other portions of the southern coastline after landfall on August 29, 2005. A Texas DPS Response Team was deployed to Baton Rouge at the request of the Federal Emergency Operations Center (EOC). The primary mission of the CIRT was to assist New Orleans police officers and fire personnel exposed to extended periods of trauma.

The team dispatched to Baton Rouge consisted of six Texas DPS troopers, one DPS mental health professional, and three DPS volunteer chaplains.

We reported to the Emergency Operations Center in Baton Rouge mid-afternoon on September 9. After receiving EOC credentials and vaccinations for hepatitis A & B, tetanus, and diphtheria, we were divided into teams of three consisting of two DPS Troopers and a chaplain or mental health professional. Each team was dispatched to one of four processing centers for incoming New Orleans police and fire personnel:

- Louisiana State Police Headquarters – Command center and staging area with meals and shelter
- Great Hall – FEMA processing center and shelter
- Fraternal Order of Police – clothing, personal items, meals, and shelter
- Bethany Evangelical Church – meals and shelter for responders

The Louisiana State Police (LSP) Headquarters is a large complex of modern buildings and facilities. The site includes the LSP Training Academy along with dormitories, cafeteria, classrooms, and physical training facilities. Louisiana state prisoners man a large laundry room used to wash and dry the clothes of first responders coming out of "The Zone" (New Orleans).

The state headquarters site also contains a secure command center and a major radio and telecommunication center. During the recovery operation, officials traversed in and out of the command center, including the Governor of Louisiana and Federal Emergency Operations Center officials.

In addition to the top-of-the-line cafeteria on campus, huge food-service tents are set up to handle the mass of personnel involved in search and rescue efforts in New Orleans some 90 miles away.

The headquarters complex is crowded with RVs housing various command centers for out-of-state police, Red Cross, and other response units from across the nation. Army National Guard and police helicopters come and go from the complex like bees filling the air with the thump-thump-thump of their rotor blades slapping at the air. Police cars from California, Georgia, Michigan, Texas, and many other states are parked in and around the large complex.

Thoughtfully, an animal shelter is set up in the laundry facility of the large dormitory. In a courteous and gentle way Louisiana State prisoners care for the pets of New Orleans officers and fire personnel. Police families have easy access to their pets during the short time they are housed at the LSP training facility.

The Great Hall serves as the processing facility for police officers and fire personnel coming out of The Zone. At one time the Great Hall was a large convention center with a massive ballroom. Now it is filled with tables for hungry and exhausted public servants. A food line is set up against the back wall. Cots and mats are lined up for temporary rest before an evacuee is moved to a more permanent shelter.

Computers line the wall across the giant ballroom from the food service line. Their monitor screens cast out a muted and bluish glow. Google Earth is on-line with current satellite images available at the touch of a keyboard. New Orleans police officers and fire personnel key in their home addresses and look with despair at their streets and homes covered with floodwaters. One retired New Orleans fireman returns every hour to look at the image of his house and mostly submerged car in the driveway. He naively hopes to see the waters receding; each time he walks away dejected.

In the foyer of the Great Hall, Red Cross and FEMA workers assist people with documentation for relief funds. Vaccinations are mandatory for everyone entering the Great Hall facility. Volunteers assist the police and fire personnel victims by escorting them to specific buses for temporary housing and security in the Baton Rouge metropolitan area.

Some are sent to the Fraternal Order of Police facility for free clothing and personal hygiene items.

Fatigued and overwhelmed New Orleans law enforcement and fire rescue personnel find respite for the first time since Katrina made landfall a week earlier. Like the thousands of citizens who lost their homes and all they owned, these public servants also lost their homes and belongings. Fortunately, most of them had sent their families inland to cities and towns prior to Katrina's arrival. All are suffering from extreme fatigue.

It does not take long for us to understand the primary issues and emotions of these faithful public servants: anger and grief.

The sources of anger included:

- Abandonment by command and line supervisors
- Fellow officers deserting their duty assignments
- Collapse of police central command
- Loss of command and line leadership created individual anger, confusion, depression, and pathological behavior
- No leadership from city officials and supervisors for days following the storm and the breach of levies
- Hundreds of available school buses flooded while waiting for evacuation orders from Mayor's office
- Criminal element preying on officers, firemen, and citizens
- Loss of personal hygiene provisions, especially for female officers trapped for long periods of time in The Zone

The sources of grief were:

- The suicide deaths of two officers
- Officer returning home finds wife and daughter drowned
- Separation from spouse, children, and family
- Sense of hopelessness mixed with anger in the midst of overwhelming chaos and lack of command support

Rev. Steve Best

- Loss of two "police partner" search and rescue dogs that died within two hours of drinking toxic water while on search and recovery duty
- Loss of home and irreplaceable family memorabilia

Although these brave men and women have many stories to tell, the five related here represent commitment amidst tragedy, commitment in the face of grief, and commitment in contrast to desertion.

Part One — Commitment upon Personal Loss

Mark, a young New Orleans police officer, stands off to the side of a FEMA processing table with a look of fatigue and grief. I ask if he is OK. The young police officer nods and, without being nudged to talk, begins to relate his grim story of loss and grief.

Mark describes one of his fellow officers, an organized and structured person due to prior military training. He praises his friend for always being on time, well prepared, and readily volunteering for assignments. However, his friend became overwhelmed by the loss of a command structure, the uncertainties created by a void in leadership, and the ever-present dangers and evils that surrounded them for days.

His face grimacing, Mark describes an unpredictable turn of events. His friend received a cell phone call from his wife who was in another city with their children. The wife told the officer their baby was sick and when she took the child to a hospital, she was told the hospital would not accept the couples' medical insurance. As in many suicide cases, one small incident often sends a person over the edge. For Mark's friend, the denial of hospital insurance was the event that triggered the officer to take his own life.

His friend's death weighs heavily on Mark's spirit. As he completes his story, his bus arrives for transport to a safe environment with clean sheets, quiet bedrooms, and hot food.

Reaching the door of the bus, he turns and smiles at me, and nods his head as if to say he will be OK. He boards the bus.

I am left with a deep feeling of sadness and prayerfulness for all the young officers who had emptied themselves for the benefit of the community and, in return, lost so much.

Part Two — Commitment in the Face of Disaster

Brenda is a New Orleans police officer. She is animated as she tells her story to a group of volunteers and peers. She and a few nursing home staff members tried to save some elderly and mentally impaired patients from rising floodwaters. She told this story:

> When I arrived at the nursing home, the few remaining staff members were preparing patients for transport to safety. The electricity had gone out with the storm several days before. The smell was horrible as we hand pumped air into tracheal tubes that had not been cleaned since the power went out. As we moved patients into the foyer, ambulances arrived and, to my amazement, the drivers refused to take the patients because they were considered low priority.
>
> My first reaction was anger. How could anyone refuse to rescue these helpless people? How could they be called low priority in their helpless condition? I commandeered a U-Haul truck and we began loading the patients. When we arrived at a hospital, we again were rejected because the hospital was over-run with people.
>
> In an attempt to reach a second medical facility, it was necessary to commandeer someone's loose fishing boat. Some way we had to traverse a flooded parking lot. One by one we brought patients to a medical refuge. Again we met resistance by medical officials. At this point, and in anger, I said to them,

"My job is to protect people and your job is to save them. Get started!"

The breach of society's basic covenant to protect the elderly and helpless resulted in them falling to the bottom of rescue priorities.

Part Three — Commitment by Refusal to Abandon Post

The four rows of folding chairs form straight lines in front of the FEMA processing table. Brittany is one of a few people in the chairs at this particular time. She and her young son are waiting patiently for FEMA immunization injections for tetanus, diphtheria, and hepatitis A and B, as well as an interview with FEMA mental health professionals to evaluate their emotional status. Despite the tired look on her face, Brittany is engaging the young boy by reading and talking to him.

She looks up at me and smiles. I introduce myself and sit down next to her. She tells me that her family is safe. However, she repeats what I heard far too often, "I lost my home. I am here to get my shots and to apply for FEMA assistance." She adds that she is eager to get back to work as a 911 operator and police dispatcher in New Orleans. This sounds a little strange since Brittany is obviously suffering from fatigue and personal loss. I ask why she feels such a strong obligation to return to her job so quickly, given her need to find housing for herself and her son. She replies; "For a week I listened to people cry for help over their telephones. I heard a trapped police officer drown in an attic. I heard elderly people crying for someone to save them – and then listened to their pitiful cries as they could no longer keep their heads above the rising water in their homes. I am needed out there. I must help those who cannot help themselves."

Seeing that she is intent on returning to a dispatch console, I summon the DPS officer partnered with me. Fortunately, he knows the phone numbers to call to relocate her to the communications center at the Louisiana State Police

Headquarters. We insist she first follow the instructions of the FEMA officials to take time to rest and renew her energy, and to find a safe environment for her son. Then she could pursue her need to return to the dispatch desk.

Looking at her young son at her side, Brittany nodded in agreement.

Part Four — Commitment to Connecting People

I walk slowly around the main ballroom of the Great Hall where police officers and firemen and/or their family members are sitting at round tables covered with white cotton tablecloths. Others stand two and three deep around the desktop computers lining the long wall. Each person wants a peek at their neighborhood accessed through the Google Earth web page.

I notice a middle-aged woman sitting at one of the tables. Rosa's head is lowered and resting on her folded arms on the table. At first I think she might be asleep, or at least resting. As I move closer I notice a slight movement in her upper body. I realize she is crying. I sit down next to her and ask if she is OK. She looks up briefly with her tear-stained face and says in three rhythmic cycles, "I'll be all right; I'll be all right; I'll be all right." It is apparent she is not all right.

Rosa returns her head to her folded arms and retreats into the darkness of her circumstances. We sit together; neither of us speaks.

I speak first. "You want to tell me about it?" She sighed and begins to tell me her story. "I am a retired New Orleans Police dispatcher. My elderly mother lives with me. We are here together."

The elderly mother returns to the table just as Rosa begins her story.

"We have lost everything – our home, our clothes, all our belongings. We have no place to go. Because I am retired from New Orleans PD, I am hopeful that I can find help here. So far I have not found much encouragement or direction."

I tell Rosa to complete the FEMA forms on the table in front of her. I describe the Fraternal Order of Police distribution center where clothing and basic hygiene products are available at no cost to her. As she is pondering this new opportunity, a member of the Eastern Star has noticed the sober drama. She comes to our table, and introduces herself. After hearing Rosa's dilemma, the Eastern Star "sister" tells Rosa that she will make certain that Rosa and her mother are taken to the Fraternal Order of Police location within the hour.

Holding hands, the four of us pray God's love for those in distress and for God's mercy in helping Rosa and her mother; we say in unison The Lord's Prayer.

Blessing both women I place the sign of the cross and a soft kiss on each of their foreheads. The two women stand up to go with their Eastern Star friend.

Several hours later I see them again from a distance in the Great Hall. Rosa, the retired dispatcher, with a smile of relief and appreciation, raises her right hand and signals me with a thumbs-up as if to say, "All is well." Her elderly mother gives a smile that only a mother can give as the two carry their few meager belongings to the next milestone of a long journey to recovery.

Part Five — Commitment for Sharing Spiritual Things

During the Critical Incident Response Team check-in at the Emergency Operations Center, a bearded man in surgical greens stands alone in the large room set aside for arriving volunteers from state and local police organizations. We are waiting in the food service line for a sandwich and soft drink. We soon will receive our housing instructions and duty station assignments. The room is crowded with police officers and troopers, social workers, chaplains, doctors, and essential personnel from across America. They fill the room with conversations reflecting uncertainties and levels of anxiety.

The man in green medical scrubs hangs back and is not involved in conversation with anyone. I notice him because he keeps staring at the "Chaplain Badge" hanging from my belt. I walk over to introduce myself. He responds, "Glad to meet you, Chaplain. My name is Sam. I'm a pathologist from Georgia."

Two days before, Dr. Sam cleared his calendar, turned his practice over to his partner, and drove to Baton Rouge to assist Katrina first responders in corpse identification. He, too, is awaiting his ID credentials at the Emergency Operations Center before being dispatched to temporary morgues in New Orleans.

Dr. Sam describes the forthcoming task of identifying the dead in New Orleans. He talks of the stress he and other medical personnel will face in the coming days and expresses his dependence on spiritual strength and courage to perform their gruesome task. It is important to him that the work of the pathologists "is done in a professional manner with dignity and respect. Each corpse was a living person only days ago. Now they are dead; trapped in houses, cars, and murky waters. No one knows who they are or where they belong."

Learning that I am from a liturgical background, Dr. Sam announces he is an Episcopal Eucharistic Minister and asks; "Do you by any chance have the elements of Holy Eucharist with you?"

I respond that I do.

Dr. Sam asks, "Would you consider sanctifying the elements and sharing your supply with me? I would like to take the sanctified elements to my assigned team's shelter. I know there will be other pathologists there who will seek The Lord's Supper."

I respond quickly, "Of course" knowing he will use the opportunities to give pastoral care with discretion and compassion. I ask him to be ecumenical in his ministry to his peers. I continue; "There are many of God's children in The Zone performing serious and gut-wrenching duties. There are a variety of spiritual beliefs in this environment of tragedy and death. We must honor all religious expressions."

The pathologist readily agrees.

Rev. Steve Best

Dr. Sam and I walk out into the parking lot. I open the trunk of the DPS sedan and retrieve my Communion kit containing the Bread and Wine. Following a prayer for the doctors and nurses that Dr. Sam will be associated with for the foreseeable future, I sanctify the bread and wine using the Words of Institution from First Corinthians:

> *...the Lord Jesus on the night when he was betrayed took a loaf of bread, and when he had given thanks, he broke it and said, "This is my body broken for you. Do this in remembrance of me." In the same way he took the cup also, after supper, saying, "This cup is the new covenant in my blood. Do this, as often as you drink it, in remembrance of me."* [20]

Clasping our hands together in a tight grip, Dr. Sam and I pray for the victims of Katrina and for those who are sent to rescue the living and recover the dead.

There we are, two men standing in a remote parking lot far away from our homes and who will never see each other again – and will probably not even remember each other's names.

We depart to our assigned duty stations knowing that the Body of Christ is to be shared in a setting reflective of the Suffering Servant – Jesus the Christ.

---

[20] 1st Corinthians 11:23b-25 - NRSV

18

Katrina and Remnant Hope

The last night our Critical Incident Response Team was in Baton Rouge, we drove to the east side of town to Bethany Evangelical Church. The church has a towering steel monument with a huge cross at the top. The monument reaches far above the busy highway and is framed in the night sky by its brilliant white surface amplified by massive floodlights. The monument creates a beacon for seekers and believers alike.

Bethany Evangelical Church is a place of respite for 125 Georgia State Police and Game Wardens. These men retreat from the floodwaters of New Orleans each evening from their mission of recovering the dead from the flooded streets and homes of New Orleans. They tell stories of bodies that have been in the water for days and how difficult it is for them to actually retrieve the bodies without them coming apart in their hands. Although there are splashes of joking mixed in their conversations, the grim reality of their tasks is far too great to ignore and the seriousness of their duty comes back across their faces like a mask. Perhaps the mask is to hide their stress and anxiety about the next day back in the dark and evil waters.

In the short time we had with them, we attempted to be good listeners and to let them tell their stories without interruption or judgment. I pray they will be given Critical Incident Stress Management debriefing therapy (Reference Appendix) when they return to their police and warden duties in Georgia. I pray they will find, in time, a sense of renewal and normalcy.

It is about seven o'clock in the evening, and we are standing on the sidewalk outside the church's fellowship hall preparing to leave for our billet. The fellowship door opens and a young woman pushes a wheelchair out the door and onto the sidewalk. The young woman is a member of Bethany Church and has finished helping serve the evening meal to the Georgia officers.

As she approaches, I notice the child in the wheelchair is impaired. Then I see the child is not only impaired, but is severely impaired. The young mother pushing the child walks directly toward me and a group of Georgia officers on her way to the parking lot. I smile and introduce myself to her, then bend down and greet the child.

Archie has no arms below his elbows. His size is that of a five-year-old even though he is nine years old. He cannot speak. He can only utter guttural sounds. His mother Katie talks about her and her husband's response to the sonograms that showed she would bear a severely impaired child – a victim of a very rare genetic defect. She confides to me that she turned to drinking, trying to escape the reality of the situation. In time her husband left her. She is caring for Archie on her own.

Although Katie was raised in a main-line denominational church, it was not until she discovered Bethany's evangelical outreach that she found a church home. In her new church home she found redemption and God's grace and faithfulness to her and her child. Now she is a giver of her time and energies to the church while caring for the child as a single mom. Clearly, she loves and adores her child as a true blessing in her life.

She and her child are not only servants of the Lord for the Georgia State troopers and wardens, but she and her son are an inspiration to the men who struggle with the repugnant tasks mandated by Katrina. They hover around Archie and Katie, giving still more of themselves. Only this time their servanthood is in the context of love, adoration, and respect.

Archie will never be a law enforcement officer. Archie will always be confined to his wheelchair and perhaps in a world with only basic communication.

But Archie has a devoted and loving mother who has escaped her addiction to alcohol and picked up the mantel of mercy and love for her son. Every one of us standing on the sidewalk that evening felt God's presence in and around Katie and Archie. Under the towering light in the sky, it was a holy moment for us that the darkness did not overcome.

In a moment of compassion, respect, and honor, I blessed Archie and placed the sign of the cross on his small forehead. Katie smiled, grateful for the blessing, and moved on down the sidewalk inspiring the heroic and exhausted public servants from their dark mission of body recovery.

A theological theme that inevitably emerges from conversations with police and fire personnel is their ever-present expression of personal faith and a need to find purpose and hope for the future. It is important that the Texas Department of Public Safety Critical Incident Response Team (CIRT) recognize the courage and commitment of the first responders based on their faith in God and in God's community. Hopefully our team empowered these public servants to become leaders in rebuilding the families, homes, and community of Katrina's devastation.

As I listen to the stories of New Orleans police officers and fire personnel, it becomes apparent they are survivors not only of Katrina and its aftermath of violence, primal behavior, and leadership abandonment, but they are also survivors of their own personal losses. These first responders are akin to the remnant so often referred to in the Old Testament when populations suffered horrific loses only to have a remnant of society become the foundation from which society and culture are rebuilt.

Rev. Steve Best

Hopefully, the brave men and women of police, fire, and EMS will see they were not defeated in the violence of Katrina. Rather, they are the remnant of what is good in New Orleans.

- *Memorable Quotes:*

- Police officer on prolonged duty in The Zone cried out: *I never thought I'd turn into an animal!*

- Volunteer: *Nobody knows what nobody's doing!*

- Plaque at Office of Emergency Management: *True heroism is not the urge to surpass all others at whatever cost, but the urge to serve others at whatever the cost.*

Contrasting Images:

- The aircraft carrier Iwo Jima (a war machine) docked next to the Carnival Cruise ship Ecstasy (a luxury machine) blended together in a mission of mercy.
- Louisiana State prison inmates providing loving care for the family pets of New Orleans police and fire personnel.

19

"He Spat in My Face"

At one time or another each of us experiences events that evoke in us anger, hatred, and a tendency toward violence. Fortunately for others, most of us do not respond in a way that would break the laws of society. We control our anger through internal fortitude even though the anger may burn inside us for awhile. Extended exasperation may at some point boil over into a verbal and/or physical confrontation with someone who was not involved in the original incident. The third party could be a spouse, a family member, or simply another individual who inadvertently triggered pent-up emotions in us.

Police officers have more than their fair share of such exasperation. But because they are sworn officers of the law, they are held to a higher standard than the rest of us. They are expected to smother the reactive emotions that would exacerbate an already volatile circumstance. Such is the case in the following story.

It is around four o'clock on a weekday afternoon. The late May afternoon sun feels more intense due to high humidity. School is out and students who live close to their middle school are walking home. By necessity, some have to cross not only a busy street, but also a parking lot adjacent to a high-volume convenience store. The neighborhood is known for its drug activity. Male and female students alike often glare at police cars that constantly patrol the area. Many students feel the ever-present police are racially profiling them and their friends.

Today a young female student is walking across the sun-baked asphalt parking lot. Loana is carrying her schoolbooks and is determined to get home quickly and without incident. She is walking alone even though there are other students and convenience store customers in the immediate area.

Unfortunately, the young girl draws the attention of a large and verbally abusive male. Melvin is over six feet tall and weighs more than 300 pounds. A big man, he towers over the young girl.

First ignoring his catcalls, then realizing she is at risk, Loana enters the store and asks for help in avoiding a threatening situation. The store manager calls 911 for her, even though he is reluctant for police to be seen on his parking lot once more. We are dispatched to the busy intersection and arrive within minutes.

I am riding with Officer Matt. He is himself a big man. In contrast to Melvin, Matt is a physically fit and intimidating force. As we exit the patrol car we see the aggressor sitting on the curb on the west side of the convenience store, where the sun hits the building unrelieved by any shade tree or other relief.

Melvin is sweating heavily. His clothes are soaked and his face and forehead are beaded with perspiration. Even though he sees us, the man continues to yell at people around him.

Back-up officers arrive and begin to interview Loana. Following her brief interview, the officers tell Loana to continue on her way home. She has nothing to fear from the man now that they are present.

Meanwhile, Melvin begins to direct his rancor at the police officers. Loud and belligerent, he enters into a monologue of denial that he verbally assaulted the "little bitch"; that he is not drunk; that he is not on crack cocaine; and that he has been minding his own business.

Evidently Loana's dad was home when she arrived, and she shared her encounter with him. Now she leads him to the convenience store and points out Melvin. They drive up next to Matt who is in a confrontational conversation with the inebriated Melvin. Loana shrinks down in the passenger seat in an attempt to avoid Melvin's attention.

Loana's father makes no attempt to be politically correct in his reaction to Melvin's verbally abusing his daughter. He begins to shout obscenities at Melvin calling him a "son-of-a-bitch" and threatening "to kill your ass if you ever even look at my girl again."

Officer Matt sternly orders the father to move on. He does, but looking back over his shoulder, he continues to curse at Melvin as he drives out of the parking lot and enters the street leading toward home.

Matt's patience is being tested to its limit. In a flash it is pushed to the edge. Melvin, in a slobbering and volatile burst of incoherent words, spits in Matt's face. Spitting at or on a police officer is considered a felony offense.

The criminality of Melvin's offensive act gives Matt cause to "take Melvin down." Instead, Matt in a lighting-fast maneuver turns the big man around, pushes his head to the hood of the police unit, bends Melvin's thumbs back against his wrists, and handcuffs him. In a calm and collected voice Matt says, "Sir, don't you ever spit on me again!" There is no anger reflected in Matt's professional and personal behavior. He arrests Melvin for public intoxication and escorts him to the back seat of his idling patrol car for transport to the county jail.

At the jail Melvin continues his belligerence. He is searched by jail personnel, booked, and placed in solitary confinement until he sobers up. Matt moves to an open computer booth and writes his report detailing the incident.

The question I often ask myself is how did Matt deal with the indignity of being spat upon? I saw him control his anger through professional training and personal internal strength. But did his extended exasperation at some point boil over into a verbal and/or physical confrontation with his family, friends, or another citizen who had absolutely nothing to do with the spitting incident? Would another incident further along his professional career pull his emotional trigger and result in an overly aggressive manhandling of a citizen?

Such human reactions are certainly within the realm of possibility.

It would not be unusual if Officer Matt experienced severe mood swings, sleepless nights, angry outbursts, or use of alcohol to compensate for the assault from Melvin's spewing mouth. It is hoped that Matt's spouse, significant other, or close friends did not try to talk Matt out of his feelings. Doing so would give him the impression that despite the good intentions of helpful people, they do not understand the complexity of an officer's patrol environment.

In contrast, a caregiver for an officer like Matt would be far more helpful by encouraging him to talk about his list of accomplishments, his kind acts toward the community, and his positive qualities as a commissioned officer of the law. Such positive outreach will reassure an officer about his/her successful management of other incidents where anger and frustration and the urge to retaliate were successfully controlled.

In our story:

- Was Melvin drunk? Yes.
- Was Melvin abusive and belligerent? Yes.
- Was Melvin likely to resist arrest? Yes.
- Did Patrol Office Matt deserve the undignified treatment he received from Melvin? No.
- Did Matt smother his anger only to vent his frustration at a later time? I don't know.
- Is the incident described in this story reflective of the deterioration of societal behavior, or was it an isolated incident on the streets of a big city?

These are questions we should ask ourselves as we strive to protect the physical and mental health of all our public servants.

20

Officer Down

The threat of injury, death, and dying are omnipresent in the shift life of a cop. At the beginning of each show-up (pre-shift briefing) a sergeant or corporal will usually say to his or her patrol officers, "Be safe." I have heard these words often as officers pick up their laptops, radios, shotguns, and other gear and leave the briefing room on their way to their police cruisers.

For me the words "be safe" are an implicit prayer. They are expressed in the context of avoiding personal injury or death in the midst of the unpredictable crises and emergency responses that occur during the span of a particular shift.

"Be safe" is also a less immediate directive, a proactive command from leadership and peers to care for one's self in working critical incident dispatches – robbery in progress, man with a gun, shots fired, family violence, disturbances calls, and high-speed chases.

"Be safe" becomes a comprehensive plea for God's presence in the certainty that serious events will occur during a 10-to-12 hour shift. "Be safe" becomes an officer's physical, emotional, and spiritual mantra that governs the short-term and long-term personal stressors caused by critical incidents.

"Be safe" becomes a reality when there is radio traffic declaring "Officer down!" For a law enforcement officer, there is absolutely nothing more powerful or that creates a more immediate response than those dreaded words.

Code 3 (lights and sirens) is instantaneous as patrol cars race to the scene of the downed officer. One of their own is hurt, maybe severely, and all attention is directed to responding to his or her plight. It is also anticipated that the perpetrators are still on scene and that rescue of the downed officer is paramount. Or, in another scenario, a patrol unit may be involved in a major wreck that has seriously injured the officer. Moreover there is the possibility that the officer is pinned in the vehicle. In any event, an active critical incident that is "going down" requires that all available resources respond.

It is Sunday night. The time is late, approaching midnight. Police Officer Rudy and I are patrolling a darkened neighborhood when dispatch assigns three patrol units to a fight occurring in the parking lot of a bar known for its patrons' boisterous behavior. Rudy immediately goes to Code 3 (overhead strobe lights and siren), knowing that we are the farthest unit away and that the first responding officers may need assistance in stopping the fight.

We are the third unit to arrive. Two officers have separated two inebriated men, and each officer is taking a statement from the combatants. Without warning, one of the men viciously pushes his interviewing officer aside and bolts toward his foe. Rudy intercepts him in a body block. Rudy and the aggressor fall to the paved parking lot. The two men land hard in all-out combat.

Unfortunately, Rudy lands on the assailant's head and his rib cage is the point of impact. Rudy, not fully realizing he is hurt, continues his effort to gain control of the unruly assailant. The officer who had been pushed aside enters the fray and the two officers handcuff the attacker.

The assisting officer jerks the man to his feet in an aggressive and authoritative manner. Rudy remains on the ground gasping for breath. He struggles to his feet and staggers toward his parked patrol car. Leaning against it, he holds his side grimacing and bending forward in obvious pain. The other two officers, loading the two drunks into their individual units for a trip to the jail, have yet to notice Rudy's plight.

I am approaching Rudy when the shift sergeant drives up. The sergeant immediately sees Rudy is in trouble, exits his patrol car and runs to his grimacing and gasping officer. The sergeant asks him; "What's wrong? Where are you hurt?" Rudy, unable to breathe or to speak, points to his left side. The sergeant unzips the fake-buttoned police shirt looking for a knife wound. He finds no such wound. The fear is growing that Rudy is suffering a heart attack. Rudy's sergeant radios "Officer down!"

It seems as though every emergency unit in the city, including fire and EMS personnel, instantaneously appear from nowhere. EMS personnel unbuckle Rudy's wide black belt with its weapon, handcuffs, flashlight, and other police-issued items attached. An EMS worker turns and hands the curled-up belt and its cluster of items to me. Carefully freeing the Velcro tabs of his body armor, they move their stethoscope across Rudy's chest to listen for an irregular heartbeat. The EMS technicians determine Rudy's heart is not the problem.

All of this is happening so rapidly that it seems only seconds before they diagnose Rudy's ribs are the source of his excruciating pain. Gently they move him to the white-sheeted gurney and carry him to the waiting EMS ambulance. Strobe lights from all the first responder vehicles pierce the dark night as the ambulance pulls away from the parking lot and disappears – its strobes and siren fading into the distance.

Handing Rudy's weapon and belt to another officer, I am given a fast ride back to my car at police headquarters. It is my intention, and the sergeant's request, to follow the ambulance to the ER at the hospital. Along the dark streets I ponder how quickly a quiet evening can turn into a chaotic night with injured officers because citizens step out of bounds in their behavior. In this case two men drinking, then fighting on the street, impacts the lives of a police officer and his family – not to mention the lives of other first responders who place themselves at risk by speeding into unknown circumstances.

Emergency room personnel acknowledge my police chaplain credentials and lead me immediately to a curtained-off triage module. I am surprised to see Rudy's wife Rachel already in the room. He has been X-rayed and is waiting for the results. We talk about the incident for the benefit of Rachel. The "defusing" (Reference Appendix) will also benefit Rudy's ability to process his traumatic experience. The conversations also will help stabilize his mental and emotional health.

The curtain opens and a young doctor in his green scrubs enters the triage cubicle with a gentle and reassuring smile on his face. Looking at Rudy, he reports; "You have a cracked rib, not broken, but cracked. I am ordering some pain meds for you, but you will be in pain for several weeks. Don't try to go to work and do not exert yourself. Ribs are slow to heal and we cannot do anything to accelerate the process – it simply takes time and rest. After six weeks or so, you will be able to return to your job. We will release you tonight. Your wife should drive you home, not the other way around. OK?"

Rudy says OK.

The doctor leaves the ER module to write a prescription for pain medications and sign the release order.

The faces of Rudy and Rachel both reflect relief over the diagnosis of a cracked rib. Their sighs of relief are in contrast to the chaotic scene just an hour before. The quick switch from routine patrol to violence is a reminder of how spouses and families are impacted by the call "Officer down."

Someone called Rachel to tell her that her beloved husband had been injured while on duty and was being transported to the hospital. In most cases a police officer will be dispatched to transport a spouse or family member to the hospital. The transport is not only a courtesy shown to a spouse but it is also to prevent further tragedy caused by a distraught driver traveling too fast to the hospital.

"Officer down" means a peace officer is a victim of some form of sudden violence. It always comes without warning.

Unlike an illness or disease where emotional adjustments are made over time, sudden violence involving a police officer is unpredictable and may occur during a routine traffic stop, domestic dispatch, or rescue event. The reality of a fatal injury is a constant worry for police spouses and families.

Police patrol units consist primarily of young men and women. Young officers:

> ...are exposed to people and events they never before dreamed of. Some of these experiences may be frightening, revolting, or disturbing, but the novelty is what counts most. Officers now have license to enter worlds that were previously forbidden to them, and some are drawn to the shadowy side of life in the way circus goers are drawn to sideshows...officers feel invincible, as though they are fulfilling a kind of hero role – protector, rescuer, powerful, brave defender of justice. [21]

It is the young officer who is most likely to become the subject of a call of an "Officer down" simply by virtue of working in an environment where danger lurks in every dispatch.

When "Officer down" becomes a death notification:

> The death of a spouse is the highest external life stressors possible. By far the greatest is the loss of the intimacy and comfort provided in marriage….The spouse was selected to be someone with whom the individual would choose to share all of his/her life….Deep emotional investment has been granted. Thus the loss is felt with extreme acuity …. Both partners develop patterns of accommodation for, and dependence on, each other. With the death of one, these patterns are completely disrupted, leaving the

---

[21] I Love a Cop – What Police Families Need to Know, Ellen Kirschman, Ph.D., The Guilford Press, New York, pp. 35-36

survivor with feelings of loneliness and a perceived inability to cope.[22]

"Officer down" does not always result in the survival of the officer. Officers die.

Only months before Officer Rudy's incident, an injured police officer from another jurisdiction died following a lengthy coma. He had been run over by a hit and run driver. The death of a police officer or trooper dramatically changes not only the lives of an officer's loved ones, but the lives of the entire police family. Numerous staff members are involved, including media-relations representatives, community liaison representatives, victim services, and administrative personnel including those who manage the storage and retrieval of data and evidence. All of these people are reminded daily of the danger *their officers* face and the finality of an officer killed in the line of duty. A line-of-duty death touches everyone.

During the investigation into the death of the officer killed by a hit-and-run driver, a homicide administrative assistant is sent to retrieve personal items his family is requesting. The staff person assigned to retrieve a specific item is Suzanne Butterfield. Suzanne tells her retrieval experience in a poem that reflects her emotional quest to honor the deceased officer and his family.

The Ring Bearer [23]
Initials and date inscribed,
Inside the gold band,
Similar to any other ring,
Once worn on the left hand.

The difference between this band
And the rest,

---

[22] <u>Death Notification – A Practical Guide to the Process</u>, R. Moroni Leash, Upper Access, Inc., Hinesburg, Vermont, p.133
[23] Suzanne Butterfield (Ret), Administrative Assistant, Homicide Div. - Used with permission

Rev. Steve Best

Was that it was retrieved
On an emergency request…

Not for a wedding,
Or any happy event,
Not from a jewelry store,
But from the basement.

The electronic page beeped out the message,
The words appeared tense,
Amid phone calls and press releases,
This message held its own suspense.

"911….Find That Ring!
45 minutes 'til funeral,
Don't come back up here
Without that thing!"

Down in the basement,
Looking through windows with bars,
Emergency mission,
People pulling out file drawers.

Brown envelopes, red evidence tape,
Plastic gloved hands
Delving frantically
For the simple gold band.

Small plastic bag,
The kind that zip locks,
Blood stained band,
The kind that silently talks.

Just a simple gold band,
An ordinary ring,
No different than any other,
Once the blood was cleaned.

Stories Of The Street

Still in plastic,
It was placed in my hand.
Was I the ring bearer now
Of the simple gold band?

How many times do we handle
Emergency requests…
Showing no emotion,
Signing off on chain of evidence.

In the grand scheme of things
Where Homicide rules,
Do the little things count?
When our roles are dual?

Do we gulp down our feelings,
Deep inside of our hearts,
And hope no one goes there,
So the crying won't start?

Returning upstairs
In the slow elevator,
Hoping no one gets on,
The time just gets later…

2nd floor stop,
The phone's ringing.
Turn sharp right,
My eyes are stinging.

"Did you get it?"
"Did you find the band?"
"Yes, sir, Sergeant," I said,
"It's in my hand."

Why did I come here?
To be a ring bearer?

Rev. Steve Best

> Could I have stayed where I was
> And never looked in the mirror?
>
> Is the need to be needed
> The driving force?
> Is it the helping desire
> That made my choice?
>
> Whatever the reason,
> I don't always like it,
> But the choice has been made.
> There's no way to fight it.
>
> What's wrong with me?
> What defines these feelings?
> After all, it was just a simple gold band.
> Once worn on [an] Officer's left hand.

Rudy did not receive a fatal injury. Rachel did not become a young widow. A cracked rib is survivable and will heal with time. Rudy will return to his career and Rachel will avoid the pain and acute grief of widowhood.

Holding hands, Rudy, Rachel, and I pray a prayer of thanksgiving and healing. We prayed for the safety and courage of the first responders who came to Rudy's aid. We prayed for the two combatants who originated the dispatch, that they will seek God's help for sobriety and a peaceful life style. We closed with the Lord's Prayer and a blessing for both Rudy and Rachel.

21

The Family

In my role as a volunteer police chaplain I have encountered scenes of tragedy, crime, and abuse. These encounters are common denominators on the streets of suburban communities and on the streets of metropolitan cities. The stories told in this book are indicative of daily street life in both cultures. The stories are indeed images of the human condition in which we all live.

The introduction of <u>Stories of the Street: Images of the Human Condition</u> says the book is not about the high drama of fast cars and drawn guns found on TV shows. Rather, the focus is on the daily life and the human emotions of officers and citizens involved in daily life. The book is about the events that occur in the ordinary life of a police officer on patrol.

The dispatches may seem routine, but in reality the officer does not know what awaits him or her when they are dispatched to a scene. The preceding stories give you an idea of the diversity of police work. However, things can and do go terribly wrong. And when incidents of tragedy, crime, or abuse go down, they invariably have a lasting impact on the officer or officers involved.

In the more traumatic stories involving death told in this book I refer to Critical Incident Stress Management (CISM) and Critical Incident Response Teams (CIRT). CISM is a group therapy approach to stress management. CIRT is a team of police peers and trained professionals that implement the CISM debriefings. Officers, chaplains, social workers must have CISM and CIRT training to participate. Both CISM and CIRT structures and procedures are outlined in the Appendix.

The theme of managing the emotional fallout of high impact incidents is for first responders to have an outlet for their emotions in a safe and trustworthy environment. The core value of CISM is the trust that expressions of grief, guilt, anger, etc. can be released without fear of reprimand or ridicule. For that reason CISM debriefings are presided over by sworn officer peers who are knowledgeable in first responder procedures and who are trained in CISM debriefing techniques. It is important to have peers who do not know the participating officers in order to avoid any personal bias. Supervisors or ranking officers of the officers involved are not permitted to be members of the Critical Incident Response Team (CIRT) and are not permitted to attend the debriefing session.

In addition to the police or trooper peers, a psychologist, licensed clinical social worker (LCSW), a victim service person, and a chaplain are members of a CIRT.

After participating in multiple CISM debriefings, I am convinced the process is a powerful tool in helping officers (especially young officers) cope with their emotions following a scene that most of us will never see in a lifetime. The days of 'don't show your emotions' following a critical incident are passing. The old way of 'being tough' and smothering one's emotional reaction to tragedy or evil is slowly giving way to effective peer counseling. It is changing into a refreshing genre that permits officers to talk about their fears and other emotions.

There are secondary results associated with participating in a CISM session. Namely, officers are better equipped to cope with issues at home without getting angry and/or depressed, and loving and caring for family at a level previously threatened by pent-up emotions. Alcohol or drug abuses become less of a crutch. The ability to meet the next challenge on the street with confidence and compassion is enhanced.

No incident is more crucial for a CIRT than a line-of-duty death of a police officer. The death pulls into focus the relationship of a deceased officer to his or her police family.

A Response Team is assembled to debrief a line-of-duty death with the deceased officer's shift partners and other officers who played a role at the death scene. The team listens carefully as shift mates talk about their experiences at the scene and their relationship with their partner. Some are angry; some are holding back deep feelings of grief; some are emotional with tears filling their eyes as they recall the incident; others are asking the WHY question.

> For many years the belief has been that human behavior is always a function of two sets of conditions, those involving the person and those involving the situation in which the person is living. As we observe grief in a social context today, it seems that our society frequently gives the message to grieving persons that their loss is not a matter of general concern. The grieving person is supposed to be *'strong'* and *'brave'* even when it is unhealthy to repress normal suffering and pain. The unfortunate consequence is that the grieving person is often left to his or her own resources at the very time those resources are the most depleted.[24]

Critical Incident Stress Management therapeutic debriefings dilute the influence of being 'strong and brave' and replaces those emotions with images of the human condition – being vulnerable to emotional heartbreak.

In one particular Response Team session, I was struck by the presence of an EMS technician and a funeral home director. Given the remote location of the death scene, the EMS

---

[24] Death and Grief: A Guide for Clergy, Alan D. Wolfelt, Ph.D., Accelerated Development, Bristol, PA, p.3

technician happened to be the first on the scene. He wanted assurance from the officers present that he had done his best to save the deceased officer. He voiced fear that he had not performed well enough to save their partner. He was reliving the scene continually in his mind, unable to focus on his job and unable to sleep.

The funeral director spoke of his friendship with the deceased officer. How he and the officer had worked similar scenes where others were the victim. Now he found his friend the victim and he lamented over the loss. The grieving peers assured both the EMS technician and the funeral director of their respect for them and how much their compassion at the scene and at the debriefing was helpful to them in working their own way through their sense of loss.

The work of first responders is implicit of the spirit as well as the body of these courageous public servants.

A line-of-duty death invariably startles and bewilders us. Why did my husband or wife have to die? Why did my partner and friend have to die? Why him or her and not me?

Harold S. Kushner writes in his book <u>When Bad Things Happen To Good People</u>[25]:

> All we can say to someone at a time like that is that vulnerability to death is one of the given conditions of life. We can't explain it any more than we can explain life itself. We can't control it, or sometimes even postpone it. All we can do is try to rise beyond the question "why did it happen?" and begin to ask the question "what do I do now that it has happened?".

Police officials will tell you that police officers and troopers work in an environment of 'family'. Sworn law officers all consider themselves part of something greater than themselves. This is the reason why police officers and other

---

[25] <u>When Bad Things Happen To Good People</u>, Harold S. Kushner, Schocken Books, New York, 1981, p.71

first responders respond en masse to an injured comrade. It is the reason that police officers will travel miles to attend a fallen officer's funeral.

The funeral for a law enforcement officer's line-of-duty death uses established police funeral protocol. The deceased officer's police chief and other senior ranking officers, political dignitaries, and chaplains are usually seated in reserved rows near the front of the sanctuary or chapel.

The service begins when an Honor Guard posts the Colors followed by the procession of the officer's family to the front pews. The family's priest, pastor, or rabbi presides over the Order of Worship following the religious practices of the family.

The mourners may well number into the hundreds from the community and from the significant number of law enforcement officers from the area, the state, and in some cases from outside the state. They gather as a family to honor one of their own.

Because visiting police officers, deputies, and troopers most often arrive as much as two hours before the service, a reception area is set up to receive them. They talk among themselves about the circumstances of the line-of-duty death. Some will open up to a chaplain and express concern for his or her own safety in a high-risk assignment. Images of the human condition again surface as personal anxiety blends itself with societal behavior.

The service concludes. The Honor Guard leads the casket and family to the waiting funeral coach and processional cars. The procession to the cemetery begins. Police escorts lead the procession, intersections are blocked off, citizens line the streets of the route, trucks and cars traveling in the opposite direction stop with most 18 - wheeler drivers getting out of their cabs and standing with their hands over their hearts. The dignity communicated to law enforcement is a testimonial to the value that the citizenry places on the men and women of law enforcement.

Rev. Steve Best

It is not unusual for the family and clergy to wait an hour or longer for the lengthy procession to reach the grave site.

The priest, pastor, or rabbi gives the burial commendation. A police bagpiper plays *Amazing Grace* as the Honor Guard folds the American Flag that covered the officer's casket. The Chief of Police presents the flag to the widow or widower.

In the distance a ceremonial rifle team fires a salute that shatters the air. From the opposite direction, dual trumpets echo each other in a mournful playing of Taps. Police and EMS helicopters do a flyby. Then silence. The air is still as everyone is caught up in the moment.

Off to the side and some distance away, a police cruiser is parked. Without warning, the voice of a female police dispatcher comes across the cruiser's loudspeaker.

"Nora 404."

Silence. Five seconds later:

"Nora 404."

Silence. Another five seconds pass:

"Nora 404."

A solemn response comes from a second loud speaker. The voice of the Chief of Police or a senior officer says:

"Nora 404, 10-42" (end tour of duty).

Silence.

The 'last call' is a simulated police radio transmission that is a traditional sendoff for a fallen officer.

Slowly and with solemnity 'the family' begins to stir and move toward their police cruisers. Each officer knows he or she will soon return to their assigned sectors and face again the realities of the images of the human condition.

The public both notices and acknowledges the tragedy of a fallen officer. What often goes unnoticed is the grief suffered by civilian (non-sworn) employees of a law enforcement agency. Civilian staff are family too. They love, admire, and cherish 'their officers'. Their grief is as great as that of the family-oriented structure of law enforcement agencies.

The violent death of an officer moved a civilian employee to express her grief in an inspired poem entitled *The Long,*

Silent Line.[26] The poem reflects the emotional significance of a police funeral.

The Long, Silent Line

As I stood on the curb
On South Congress Avenue
On the afternoon of February 21, 2001,
I watched a long line of police and sheriff vehicles,
With flashing lights,
And silent faces,
Gazing out from inside
The slowly moving vehicles
Passing by me.

I thought,
As I stood close
To Fire Department personnel
Who were guarding intersections
And keeping traffic flowing,
That I was surely invisible
To that passing line of cars.

I was dressed in black,
APD ID around my neck,
Hand over my heart,
For as long as it took
For those thousand vehicles
To pass by.

I felt my heart pounding
Underneath my hand
Which was held tightly in place
Over my heart.
I felt as many emotions

---

[26] Suzanne Butterfield, Administrative Assistant (Ret), Homicide Division - Used with permission

Rev. Steve Best

As there were vehicles that passed by.

I didn't know the
Deceased sheriff deputy.
So I wondered what it was
That caused me
To feel so deeply
About his passing.

I realized what I felt
Was a profound loss.
What if he had been one of
My detectives?
What if he had been one of
My sergeants?
What if he was my Lieutenant?
What if he was my Commander?

What if this man,
Who was with us no more,
Had been one of my new law enforcement family,
Who had accepted me
To work closely with him
As one of his own?

What if I had lost
One of the few people in my life
Who had taken a chance on me
And accepted me
Just as I am?

It would be like losing myself,
After struggling with
Having been lost
For so many years.

It would be a painful hole of sorrow.

Stories Of The Street

It would be the loss
Of never having said,
From day to day,
How much we depend on
And believe in
Each other.

It would be the loss
Of the strong place
We build here
From day to day
Together.

It would be the loss
Of a place of acceptance
And gratitude –
A close place,
Where we come to know each other –
Maybe better than our own families know us.

It would be the loss
Of knowing and accepting…
And then just going on.

So on that curbside,
Feeling invisible and small,
In the afternoon haze,
With the occasional crying of babies
In the background,
Held by their mothers,
And with more than a few irate motorists,
Inconvenienced by held-up traffic,
Never giving a thought to the uniforms
Who serve them,
Only wanting the uniforms there
When it is convenient for them…
Angry at the motorcycle cop

Rev. Steve Best

        Who had the "nerve"
        To order them
        In solemn voice command,
        DO NOT CROSS…

        In the middle of this procession,
        I catch the glance of a sorrowful face
        Riding inside the long line of cars.
        A glance that meets my eyes,
        And holds them just long enough
        To nod their head
        In my direction,
        Acknowledging my presence,
        And mouthing the silent outline
        Of the words
        "Thank You."

        In those few seconds
        I feel visible
        And appreciated
        And very much a part
        Of the long, silent line.

My prayer is that <u>Stories of the Street: Images of the Human Condition</u> has inspired the reader to search for a Divine Presence in the context of how each reader understands God.

Appendix

In <u>Stories of the Street: Images of the Human Condition</u> there are multiple references to Critical Incident Stress Management (CISM) and Critical Incident Response Teams (CIRT). The two therapeutic approaches are designed to provide a confidential and secure environment for first responders to reduce the emotional impact of horrific scenes of injury, death, and destruction. The underlying theme of CISM is to find emotional relief through dialogue with peers who understand and who themselves have experienced similar traumatic critical incidents.

CISM and CIRT have been initiated and refined over the past decade by metropolitan, rural, and state law enforcement agencies. The thesis is to gather seasoned police officers/troopers who are not from the same sector, district, or sub-station of the first responders seeking help. In addition to the peers, a mental health professional, a victim service representative, and a chaplain complete the membership of a Critical Incident Response Team (CIRT). It is paramount that the Critical Incident Response Team members do not outnumber the officers/first responders seeking help.

In order for those needing/seeking help to talk freely about their feelings in a confidential environment, supervisors are not allowed in the debriefing room. The session is not a critique of what a first responder did or did not do at the scene. The session is not a formal Review Board, nor is it a platform for discipline. The debriefing is structured to restore the damaged emotional health of first responders negatively impacted by a critical incident.

The following abbreviated outline for CISM and CIRT training is taken from the Texas Department of Public Safety (Texas DPS) training manual for Critical Incident Response Teams. The CISM and CIRT programs were initiated and refined within the Psychological Services Division of the Texas DPS. Dr. Frances Douglas, Psy.D. serves as the DPS Staff Psychologist. She supervises both programs including the statewide Chaplain Program. Dr. Douglas has approved the use of the CISM outline for <u>Stories of the Street: Images of the Human Condition</u>.

Critical Incident Stress Management:

- Goal to reduce symptoms, prepare people for stressful events, and achieve adequate level of resolution
- Not therapy but peer support and education
- Uses a variety of tools and methodologies

Possible Critical Incidents

- Line of duty death
- Mass casualty disaster
- Death of a child
- Death or injury of co-worker
- Natural disasters
- Repeated serious or traumatic events
- Suicide of co-worker
- Workplace violence
- Prolonged mission with or without death
- Excessive media interest
- Any unusually stressful event or situation

Critical Incident Response Team (CIRT)
- Facilitated by CISM trained mental health professional
- Group process of people directly involved in a critical incident
- CISM trained occupational peers – out-of-area officers/troopers not involved with incident
- Assisted by CISM trained clinical chaplain

Best Time for CISM / CIRT Debriefing

- Between 24 and 72 hours is ideal
- Earlier in some extraordinary cases
- Later when the requirements of the situation warrant later intervention
- Loses effectiveness with increased time after the incident

CISM Confidentiality

- Turn off pagers and cell phones
- No notes or records kept
- No cameras, recorders, or notes
- Only those involved in specific Critical Incident and CIRT belong in session
- No rank present

- Put aside hierarchical relationships
- What is said here stays here
- Not for investigation or mission critique
- Talk about YOUR own experience and reactions
- Seven-step process with beginning, middle, and end
- Follow-up may be indicated for group or individuals

Seven Phases of CISM / CIRT Debriefing

- Introduction
- Fact
- Thought
- Reaction
- Symptoms
- Teaching
- Re-entry

1. Introduction Phase

- Introduce CIRT leader
- Point out CIRT members
- Explain purpose of meeting
- Describe what a debriefing is
- Explain what will happen
- Provide reassurance for their concerns
- Encourage mutual help and respect for others
- Speak for yourself, not others
- People do not have to speak except for three question (see Fact Phase)
- All participants required to stay for entire CISM session

2. Fact Phase

- These three question asked of **each** participant:
  - ✓ Who are you?
  - ✓ What was your role in the incident?
  - ✓ What happened from your point of view?

3. Thought Phase

- Purpose
  - ✓ Move deeper into the situation

- ✓ Allow participants to look at their motivations and impressions
- ✓ Transition from cognitive to emotional

- Questions to **group**:

  - ✓ What was your first thought when you got off "auto-pilot" mode?
  - ✓ What was your main thought during the incident? OR
  - ✓ What was your most prominent thought as you handled the incident?

4. Reaction Phase

   - Allows deepest recall of event
   - Symbolism of event may be revealed
   - Most group and peer support possible
   - Where re-framing and re-naming takes place
   - May be the longest part of CISM debriefing
   - Questions to **group**:

     - ✓ What was the worst thing about this event for you?
     - ✓ What part of this incident would you like to erase if it were possible?
     - ✓ What part of this event was the most difficult for you or caused you the most distress?

5. Symptoms Phase

   - Spirituality exists in and through symptoms of critical incident emotional responses

   - Question to **group**:

     - ✓ What cognitive, physical, emotional and behavioral symptoms did you experience at the scene?
     - ✓ Next few days?
     - ✓ Leftover now – reoccurring?

6. Teaching Phase

   - Always provided by CIRT members
   - Talk about symptoms you experienced or currently experience
   - Suggested question to **group**:

- ✓ Was there one thing that happened that helped you or made the situation a bit easier to tolerate?

- Topics for healing

  - ✓ Diet
  - ✓ Exercise
  - ✓ Alcohol and drugs
  - ✓ Contact with family
  - ✓ Contact with friends
  - ✓ Group social network
  - ✓ Calling for professional help if necessary
  - ✓ When to call for help
  - ✓ Recovery is typical
  - ✓ Debriefings may cause some initial pain, but there is more pain without them
  - ✓ Review CISM themes of peer support

7. Re-Entry Phase

   - Questions to **group**:

     - ✓ Are there any questions you want to ask?
     - ✓ Any statements anyone wants to make?

   - Both participants and CIRT members interact
   - Only CIRT members make summary comments
   - Information and/or issues already discussed may be re-visited
   - New subjects or issues may surface

8. Follow-up Phase

   - One-on-one contact
   - Defusing (see Defusing)
   - Additional debriefings
   - Phone calls
   - Peer visits
   - Chaplain visits
   - Peer or Chaplain ride-along
   - Referral to agency or local mental health professional

Ask if participants would like to close with prayer.

Critical Incident Stress Management Defusing:

- A Defusing is a short version of CISM debriefing
- Small group intervention after a traumatic incident
- Designed to lessen Critical Incident Stress
- Facilitated by CISM / CIRT trained peer or mental health professional
- Takes place within the shift working the incident
- On or near the workplace
- 20-40 minutes in duration

Goals of a Defusing:

- Lessen impact of event
- Restore to normal duties
- Screen group for possible further intervention
- Prepare first responder to return home with lighter emotional burden

Three Phases of Defusing:

- Introduction
- Exploration
- Information

1. Introduction Phase:

   - Welcome and why we are here
   - Short session on emotions
   - We have learned that defusing helps people after a traumatic event

2. Exploration Phase

   - What happened?
   - Describe the event from your perspective
   - What was it like for you?
   - What other things were going on around you?
   - What part are you having difficulty with right now?

Rev. Steve Best

3. Information Phase

- Normalize the event in terms of participants' occupation and in terms of the emotional reaction to a stressful event
- Educate about CISM, trauma and stress management
- Discuss resources for emotional/mental healing
- Offer one-on-one defusing

Ask if participants would like to close with prayer.

CPSIA information can be obtained at www.ICGtesting.com
Printed in the USA
LVOW060458150413

329086LV00003B/154/P